CHILDREN OF LIGHT

Children of Light

AARON EBY

FIRST FRUITS OF ZION

For my companion

Rachel Zisa

תורת חסד על לשונה

FIRST FRUITS OF ZION

Copyright © 2023 First Fruits of Zion. All rights reserved.
Publication rights First Fruits of Zion, Inc.
Details: ffoz.org/copyright

Publisher grants permission to reference short quotations (less than 400 words) in reviews, magazines, newspapers, web sites, or other publications in accordance with the citation standards at ffoz.org/copyright. Requests for permission to reproduce more than 400 words can be made at ffoz.org/contact.

First Fruits of Zion is a 501(c)(3) registered nonprofit educational organization.
Printed in the United States of America

ISBN: 978-1-941534-67-0

The prayer text in this book, which includes scriptural passages, is an original translation by the author.

All other scriptural quotations, unless otherwise noted, are from the Holy Bible, English Standard Version®, copyright © 2001 by Crossway Bibles, a publishing ministry of Good News Publishers. Used by permission. All rights reserved.

Also cited: The New American Standard Bible®, © 1960, 1962, 1963, 1968, 1971, 1972, 1973, 1975, 1977, 1995 by The Lockman Foundation. Used by permission.

Cover design: Anne Mandell

Quantity discounts are available on bulk purchases of this book for educational, fundraising, or event purposes. Special versions or book excerpts to fit specific needs are available from First Fruits of Zion. For more information, contact ffoz.org/contact.

First Fruits of Zion

PO Box 649, Marshfield, Missouri 65706-0649 USA
Phone: (417) 468-2741
Website: ffoz.org

Comments and questions: ffoz.org/contact

Contents

Foreword...ix

Introduction.. 1

The Hidden Light 7

Light of the World.................................... 21

The Light Within..................................... 35

Separating from the Darkness 49

Perfect Light.. 63

Basking in the Light 77

Conclusion.. 89

FOREWORD

Every generation of God's people struggles to maintain the light of faith and pass it on to the next generation. Jews and Christians alike have made every effort to raise their children to be people of faith, and this task has never been easy. In that sense, the struggle we face today is one we share with all of God's people from the time of Abraham.

In another sense, our struggle is unique. Human nature is the same, but the world we live in would be unrecognizable to past generations. Social media has forever altered how we present ourselves to the world and the way we connect with each other. Our carefully curated social media feeds give us a false, unrealistic perspective on the state of the world, our relationships, and even ourselves.

Young people come of age in a world of illusion. Carefully edited photos of professional models provoke young women to develop eating disorders. Artificially masculine influencers convince young men that women are objects to be fought over and won. A real danger presents itself: The spiritual journey will become merely an accessory, another component of a completely fake life, and just another identity label. Appearing to be a spiritual person is easier than *being* a spiritual person, and pretending is easier than ever.

Because of the ease with which we can artificially portray ourselves in digital spaces, young people today are perhaps more acutely aware of the importance of authenticity than generations before them. They understand that a spiritual journey—a spiritual life—must be authentic, and they, like anyone else, long for that authenticity. They long to be true to themselves and true to their beliefs.

In the six short chapters of *Children of Light*, Aaron Eby cuts to the heart of what it means to be an authentic disciple of our Master, Yeshua. Every one of us was born into this world with a mission: to seek the hidden light of God's presence and to display that light to others through righteous living and acts of kindness. This mission leaves no room for artificiality or pretense.

Aaron expertly describes the problems of posturing and hypocrisy, explaining why it is so easy to fall into the trap of merely acting religious and how easy it is for others to sense this hypocrisy. In the end, our spiritual journey is at its most authentic when we admit that all the good we bring into the world is a reflection of God's hidden light:

> Let your light shine before others, so that they may see your good works and give glory to your Father who is in heaven. (Matthew 5:16)

When we reveal the hidden light, we reveal something real—the character of God himself. When we are successful in our mission, and others see that light, we spread awareness of what is real and what is false. We awaken others to the reality that God exists and that he desires a relationship with us.

In a sense, this entire world is artificial. God has concealed himself; the light he created on the first day has been hidden away. We must work to cultivate an awareness of his presence. We must learn to see through the illusion that he is absent and realize that he is always with us, that he desires to have an authentic relationship with us, and that this world is merely an opportunity to prepare for the World to Come.

I pray that this book will help people of faith realize that they are not children of this present age but children of light—spiritual beings born with a spiritual purpose. I pray that anyone who reads this will take hold of the mission they were placed here to accomplish and that, in the process, they will truly come to know both God and themselves.

Boaz Michael
JERUSALEM 5783

Introduction

I was once a teenager. I was a nerdy kid, into science and computers and stuff like that. I played the trombone and was in the marching band. I had a few friends in school, mostly other nerdy kids, but I was not a popular kid. I was even bullied a little bit. Fortunately, I hit puberty early and took some karate classes, which helped. I'm still a nerd, and my friends are mostly other nerds.

As a teenager, the hub of my social life was my church, especially the youth group. That's where my real friends were. My family attended an Assemblies of God church for most of my young life. My parents, whom I greatly admire, taught me two distinct ideas about faith. First, they have always been strong believers; they love God and taught me to know and love God. Second, they taught me to think critically about everything, not to automatically buy into whatever was being presented at the pulpit. They encouraged me to seek authenticity.

The main reason we attended the Assemblies of God church was that it had a good youth program. Assemblies of God is a Pentecostal denomination. We Pentecostals looked at the book of Acts and saw the miracles happening in the first century, how people were filled with the Holy Spirit and prophecy, and how they would speak other languages under the influence of the Spirit. We thought that's how church should be today. So we tried to model our church after that.

But something bothered me; all the talk about supernatural gifting seemed like hype. We were trying to force something spiritual to happen, but it was missing authenticity. I wondered what the first-century believers had that we didn't.

I have some Jewish ancestry, but my family knew nothing about Judaism. We knew that Jesus was Jewish, but that's about it. Like almost all churches, our church took communion. The way our church did this would be familiar to many. We got a tiny cracker and an itsy-bitsy plastic cup of grape juice, which I am sure was watered down. We read a couple of Bible verses, took a moment to feel bad about our sins, and then ate the cracker and drank the juice.

One day, my dad came home with a box of matzah and a bottle of juice. He had just learned about Passover and had discovered that communion was supposed to be based on a seder. He told us how full of meaning the Passover meal was and that each element carried deep symbolism. He gave us each a big piece of matzah and a full glass of grape juice. He told us that "communion" was originally a full meal.

That ruined me. Every time we did communion in our church after that, I would roll that little cracker around in my fingers and imagine being at a Passover meal with a table loaded with food, each element carrying some profound significance. The tiny cracker was a fitting symbol for the tiny amount of information I had. I knew I was missing something huge and wanted to know more.

The questioning mindset my parents gave me, plus a lot of curiosity about having some Jewish ancestors set me on a path in my early twenties that eventually led to Messianic Judaism. When I found it, I knew that this was where God wanted me. I met my wife, Rachel, at a Messianic congregation; the rest is history.

My life has been a spiritual quest. Even after getting involved with Messianic Judaism, I've gone through many phases and ways of thinking. I've hit a few spiritual dead ends that forced me to turn around and start looking at things differently. Even though I have had to change, grow, learn, and relearn many times, God has always been there with me, guiding me. This lifetime is too short to learn all that I wish to know. And yet, I'm amazed at what HaShem has allowed me to learn about the meaning of the Bible, why he created the world, and why Yeshua is so misunderstood.

I'm writing this book to help you. Each one of you, like me, is on a quest. My job is to show you as much of the big picture as possible. I want to help you gain a sense of perspective and direction, and I want you to be able to avoid some of the pitfalls I encountered. I want to encourage you to question, wrestle with, and sift through the information you have gained so far in your life so you can arrive at the ultimate destination: knowing God. I'm not here to make you believe in God; there's no point in believing in God if you don't know him. But once you know God, it's hard not to believe in him.

I first presented the ideas in this book at Camp Tzadi on Ice, an event held over New Year's 2022. The theme of that camp was Children of Light. This theme was chosen with all frankness; within these words lies an incredible significance that we are about to explore together. The phrase "Children of Light" comes right from the Bible—several places in the Bible, actually—and it's talking about you. It's an identity. This identity comes from a purpose God gave each of you to fulfill. There is no guarantee that you will fulfill it; the whole point of this life is that it's a choice, or really, a relentless series of many choices.

The fact that you are a child of light is the most important thing about you. I wish we talked about this more. It's more important than being American, Israeli, Messianic, Christian, Jewish, Gentile, a boy, or a girl. It gets to the core of being a human soul. It goes all the way back to God deciding you should exist.

I've composed these chapters to guide you along a path. As I prepared this material, I thought of it as a story, like a novel with six chapters, and you're the main character. I start each chapter by introducing a problem or a goal and then take you through the steps needed to solve the problem. Each chapter builds on the previous one.

As we go through the chapters, one might resonate more with where you are right now on your journey. Pay attention and see if you get some insight to help you overcome your current struggles. On the other hand, these chapters are not necessarily in a rigid order. They present issues we all constantly struggle with, so they apply to each of us every day.

Be prepared for some deep thoughts. Some of these chapters lay out mysterious spiritual ideas; this is especially true for the first one. But bear with me; eventually, we will get into practical instructions about how to live. This book will challenge you to improve as a person. To be honest, even as I prepared this material, I felt God challenging me to improve myself.

Here's a quick preview of the chapters:

- ★ Chapter 1 is about the "hidden light." Our tradition tells us that in the beginning, God created spiritual light but stashed it away as a reward for the righteous. We will learn that story, its meaning, and how it applies to our lives.
- ★ In chapter 2, we will learn how to seek God in this world when he is hidden, and we will talk about why being a disciple of Yeshua matters at all.
- ★ Chapter 3 discusses the challenge of being a spiritual person and the right and wrong ways to help others see God's light.
- ★ In chapter 4, which was originally taught on Shabbat, we will learn directly from that week's Torah portion and a people surrounded by one of the most wicked societies in history about how to keep from being overcome by the darkness.

- ★ In chapter 5, we will talk about how not to fall into the trap of becoming a religious hypocrite or pretender.
- ★ Finally, in chapter 6, we will discuss why God wants you in this world and the impossible task he wants you to accomplish.

I developed this material to help you. My goal is not to dazzle you with my extensive vocabulary and mystify you with incomprehensible ideas. If you don't understand something, that's my fault for not communicating well.

I want to bless you so that you will discover and connect with God on a deeper level. Thank you for taking the time to read this book, and I pray it will help you on your quest.

Aaron Eby

CHAPTER 1

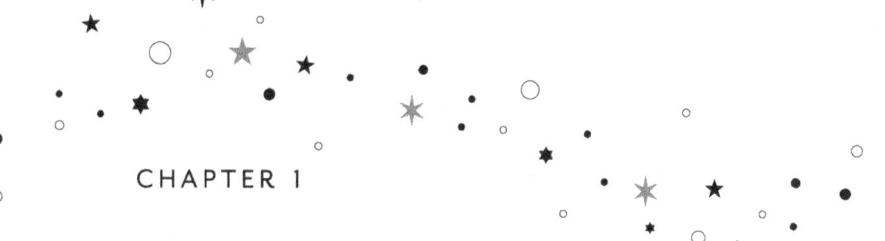

THE HIDDEN LIGHT

Let's read the beginning of the creation story from the Bible. As you read these few verses, I want you to picture each event as literally as possible:

> In the beginning, God created the heavens and the earth. The earth was without form and void, and darkness was over the face of the deep. And the Spirit of God was hovering over the face of the waters. (Genesis 1:1-2)

WHAT KIND OF LIGHT?

Take a moment to close your eyes and visualize everything you just read. Hold the images in your mind.

Now let's read the next verse. "And God said, 'Let there be light,' and there was light" (Genesis 1:3). Before you read, "there was light," what were you picturing? Did you imagine even a little bit of light? If so, you might need to revise your mental image. Imagine total darkness.

Before God said, "Let there be light," the text says there was already darkness, and it was over the face of the deep. It makes sense for darkness to be there since darkness is the absence of light. But why does it say that the darkness was in a specific place—over the face of the deep? If there is no light, then the darkness should be everywhere.

Go back to your mental image. God said, "Let there be light," and there was light. Picture this: the shapeless and empty earth, the deep, God's Spirit hovering over some watery surface. Then, suddenly, there's light.

Where is that light coming from? Light is always moving. It moves at the speed of light. Light as we know it always has an origin, whether it be a campfire, a lightbulb, or the sun. The only reason you can see any object is that photons started somewhere and then bounced off that object in the perfect trajectory to pass through the lens of your eye and hit your retina.

In your mental picture of creation, where is that light coming from? It can't be coming from the sun or the stars. The sun, moon, and stars did not exist yet. It wasn't until the fourth day of creation that "God set them in the expanse of the heavens to give light on the earth" (Genesis 1:17). If God already made light, what need is there for the sun, moon, and stars?

Back to our mental image of creation. We just pictured God creating light. Now it says:

> God saw that the light was good. And God separated the light from the darkness. (Genesis 1:4)

The light was good? What does that mean? Good for what? If God separated the light from the darkness, it means that at first, the light and the darkness were mixed up. Is that how you visualized it, light and darkness mixed together? What would it mean for light and darkness to be separated? In our world, light and darkness are not entirely separate. We have lights in dark places and shadows in bright places. We have murky light, diffused light, and faint light. We even have blacklight and infrared light. When I think about this, I have two questions about the creation story:

1. What kind of light is the light of the first day of creation?

2. What does it mean that God separated light from darkness?

Before we answer those, let's raise one more question. This one is from Paul's letter to the Colossians. The Colossians were Gentile disciples of Yeshua who lived in a city called Colossae. Paul wrote them a letter and told them he was praying for them. Then he said something strange. He said he was "giving thanks to the Father, who has qualified you to share in the inheritance of the saints in light" (Colossians 1:12).

Don't get thrown off by the word "saints"—it just means "holy ones." Now, imagine it's time for you to receive your inheritance. Maybe you hope you're getting a house, a nice car, a savings account, or even some precious family heirlooms. But no, here's your inheritance: it's light. Here's my third question: What does it mean to inherit light?

WHY DO YOU EXIST?

Have you ever thought about how many galaxies, planets, and stars there are in the universe? Because the universe is expanding, some of them are traveling away from us so fast that even if we had a light-speed spacecraft, we would never reach them. The little we have seen, here on earth, in our own solar system and through telescopes, is beautiful beyond description. It grieves me to think about the unfathomable number of beautiful creations that humans will never lay eyes on!

Other animals experience creation, but humans are the only creatures, as far as we know, that are aware that they are experiencing creation. We are the only ones who purposely seek to understand the universe. What's more amazing is that humans are not just inside creation—they are creation. To put a twist on something Carl Sagan said: Humanity is a way for creation to know itself.

This is not just a fascinating idea; it's why we exist. To know creation—but even more so, through knowledge of creation, to know the Creator. Humanity's purpose is to understand, know, and experience God and have the truth of the universe revealed.

But we have a problem. With this lofty purpose, our soul is riding on a meat robot, capable only of processing a fraction of its surroundings using the blob of gray tissue we call our brain. Brains are easily distracted by the demands of the meat robot—like staying alive. Your soul wants to behave like a spiritual being, but it's hard most of the time. That makes you frustrated with yourself, feeling guilty about your inability to be spiritual or to stay committed.

None of this is an accident. God made you a physical being. He put the soul on the meat robot, with all its needs, urges, and limitations. But if knowing him is the point of life, why did he make it so difficult? Why did he make an enormous universe to reveal his glory only to let us see a tiny sliver of it?

You were created because God wants to reveal himself to you. Not humanity, *you*. He is hidden from you now, but he is waiting for the right moment to reveal everything. And I mean everything.

To understand this, we need to learn the story of the hidden light. It's a deep idea. We'll see why it's worth the effort to continue pursuing God to the end. We will learn how important it is to have a broad perspective on life rather than a short-sighted one. Finally, we will discuss the practical implications of these lofty ideas.

THE STORY OF THE HIDDEN LIGHT

We are children of light. As children of light, we are a people. We are a tribe, and we have a backstory. Let me tell you our story.

Our God is the God of everything. He didn't just create everything that has ever existed and will ever exist; he created the idea of everything and the idea of existence.

One of God's first creations was light. But it wasn't the light we usually think of. Light as we know it—photons erupting from stars, twisting through lenses, and bouncing off objects—is only a metaphor. It symbolizes the true light our God created at first. What was this original light?

We children of light have an ancient tradition about this. I will tell you the story from the words of our sages:

> If light was created on the first day, why is it written, "God set [the luminaries] in the expanse of the heavens [to give light on the earth] ... and there was evening and there was morning, the fourth day"? [But the light of the first day is not the natural light of the luminaries.] The light that the blessed Holy One created on the first day allows a human to see from one end of the universe to the other.
>
> When the blessed Holy One considered the generation of the flood and the Tower of Babel and perceived how corrupt their deeds would be, he stashed away the light. As Job 38:15 says, "From the wicked their light is withheld." But for whom did he stash away the light? For the righteous people of the future, as it says, "God saw that the light was good (tov)." *Tov* refers to one who is righteous, like Isaiah 3:10 says, "Tell the righteous that it shall be *tov*."
>
> When the light saw that it was stashed away for the righteous, it rejoiced. As it says in Proverbs 13:9, "The light of the righteous rejoices." (b.*Chagigah* 12a)

That's our backstory, and it raises some questions. You don't have to be a scientist to see the problem with light enabling a person to see from one end of the universe to the other. You can't see from one end of the universe to the other because the light isn't bright enough; there is always something in the way. If you had light that could pass through everything, what would you see? Nothing, because everything would look transparent.

We're thinking too physically. The point is that the hidden light is something that allows you to perceive all creation. It enables you to take in everything God made and to understand the universe with full context and detail. You would see not only space but also time, from beginning to end. It allows you to see things that can't be illuminated by physical light: the soul, consciousness, the spiritual world, and truth itself.

With this hidden light, you will grasp the reasons for everything—all the contradictions, ironies, and injustices that infect this world. Once you see with this light, you can wrap your mind around the biggest truth of all. What truth is this?

Moses told the Israelites: "To you it was shown, that you might know that the LORD is God; there is no other besides him" (Deuteronomy 4:35). Moses doesn't just mean that there is no other God. *Ein Od Milvado*, "there is no other," means there is nothing else but him. When you behold the hidden light, you will see that everything that exists does so only because God consciously wills it at every moment. That means that our existence is nothing like his—so different that we don't exist at all compared to his existence. It's only him.

God stashed this light away. He hid it, which is why we feel like we exist, and why there is always something in our way that makes it hard to see him. He hid the light so that free will could exist. In the presence of that light, there can be no choices.

God's process of creation is one act of separation after another. Day 1: He separated between light and darkness. Day 2: He separated the water above from the water below. Day 3: He separated the dry land from the sea. And so on: He separated each plant and animal into various kinds.

He also created souls of different kinds. Right now, all these different souls interact with each other. People in this world are not yet sorted; the righteous and wicked co-exist. God is hidden, and in this empty space, each soul feels as though it exists on its own and can express its own will, its free choice. The space for free will allows each soul to show its true nature. The souls who choose good will be reunited with the hidden light. Yeshua describes this soul-separation process in many of his parables.

This is what the sages meant when they said the light is stashed away for the righteous in the World to Come. The holy souls who choose good are qualified to receive that light as their inheritance. That light is their home, their kingdom, their destiny. Let me read again what Paul wrote to the Colossians. He told them, "[We are] giving thanks to the Father, who has qualified you to share in the inheritance of the [holy ones] in light" (Colossians 1:12). Paul is in awe that through Messiah, it's not only Jews who are destined to inherit the light, but all holy souls. Our inheritance is the same.

THE REWARD IS WORTH IT

Once, I went to an amusement park, and there was a ticket booth and an admission gate at the entrance. Inside the park were roller coasters, waterslides, exhilarating rides, and attractions of all kinds, something for all ages. But outside the gate, I noticed a little horsey ride, like you might find at a grocery store or shopping mall. It was a little horse; you put in a dollar, and it bumps up and down for about sixty seconds. I wondered what kind of evil parent would bring their little kid to an amusement park, set them on the horsey ride outside the gate, and make them think that was all there was.

Now imagine you're a kid in line. Tickets for the amusement park cost fifty dollars, and you have fifty dollars in your hands. You don't know what's on the other side of the gate, but you know that you have been standing in this boring line in the sweltering summer sun for what feels like an eternity. You see that there is no one in line for the horsey ride. Instead of waiting in line, you could ride that thing fifty times.

This life is the line outside the amusement park. Or, as one rabbi said in an ancient book of wisdom called *Pirkei Avot*, "This world is like an entryway before the World to Come. Get yourself ready in the entryway so that you can enter the banquet hall."

The hidden light is more than a trophy you get at the end of your life. It is your life. It is the point of existence. The World to Come is the real world, the purpose of creation. Your life hasn't even started yet. When a kid is waiting in line, they think it's taking forever, but once they get inside, they forget about standing in line.

That's what this world is. It's not the real world; it's only the admission gate! Don't spend your fifty dollars on the horsey ride!

This world is a test, a process of sifting souls, but don't think God is trying to keep you out. He wants you in the World to Come; he wants to give you the hidden light; otherwise, he wouldn't have created you in the first place. You belong there.

God created you as the person you are because he wanted a soul to go through everything you will go through, to overcome all your difficulties and challenges and circumstances, and from within that darkness to seek him and attain the hidden light. This is your mission in life and why your soul was attached to your specific meat robot.

You constantly have choices between reward in this world or reward in the future world. Most people will choose an immediate reward and, in doing so, live a life that is much like that of an animal.

But not us. By the grace of God, we are different. We have become children of light. What does that mean? Being a "child of light" means that the hidden light is your true home, your ultimate destination, your reward. You are not a child of this world. Being a child of light means you are part of a family and a tribe that transcends time and space, and as a part of this family, the hidden light is your inheritance.

EXPAND YOUR PERSPECTIVE

Let's think about the practical implications of this. This world is a test and an entryway, and its purpose is to prepare you for the main event. The main event is the revelation of God, the universe, and all understanding—to feel a connection with the source of everything, to know the creator, your Father, who loves you. What does all this imply about how we should live our lives today? If you keep this truth at the forefront of your mind, it will change everything about the choices you make.

First, it will help you cope with the struggles you face day to day. You have schoolwork, and you are trying to keep your grades up. You want people to like you, and you want to fit in. You are thinking about your looks and your body and how others perceive you. There are so many things you want to do. Maybe you have conflicts with your parents, siblings, or other family members. You're wondering who you will marry or just longing for companionship. You are concerned about pursuing a career and how you will make a living, or maybe you have a job right now, and it's tough.

Spoiler alert: You will never get to the point where those struggles go away. They get bigger as your life moves on. But the good news is that when your mind is focused on the World to Come, the kingdom, the difficulties aren't as overwhelming. This is the meaning of Psalm 16:8, one of the most often used verses in Jewish meditation: "I have set the LORD always before me; because he is at my right hand, I shall not be shaken."

Second, keeping your sights on the World to Come will help keep you from getting distracted by cheap pleasures. The horsey ride. This world offers a lot of horsey rides and easy thrills that are not worth it in the end.

Third, you will realize how short your life is and how important it is to use your time wisely. This world may not be the real world, but it has one natural resource that is scarce in the World to Come:

choice. The hiddenness of God's presence is painful, but it turns this world into a goldmine of opportunity. One choice to serve God or to repent in this world is enormously valuable in the World to Come. Every second of the day is an opportunity to gather this treasure and store it up for yourself in the future. Don't waste a single moment.

In Luke 16, Yeshua taught a parable about a wealth manager. Rich people hire wealth managers and give them access to their money. Wealth managers know how to use money to make more money by loaning it out, investing in businesses, and so on. The rich person doesn't really care what the wealth manager does with the money, as long as it keeps increasing. The manager gets complete control of the bank account.

In this story, the rich man hears a rumor that his wealth manager is skimming funds and using them for personal expenses. Were the rumors true? We never find out. But the manager knows that it's just a matter of time before he will be fired. He doesn't have much money of his own. He's not fit for manual labor. He has no other useful skills. He is about to be as poor as dirt, but he has access to an enormous bank account for the next few hours. He can't steal the money; the courts will make him give it back. He needs to find a legal maneuver to leverage his situation so that he will be sitting pretty after he is fired.

As the wealth manager, it's his job to set the terms on loans. So, one by one, he goes to business partners who have taken out big loans and slashes their debt in half. Just like that, he has a bunch of rich friends who owe him a big favor.

You might imagine his boss will be upset when he finds out what happened, but Yeshua tells us that the rich man understands that business is business and responds, "Well played":

> The master commended the dishonest manager for his shrewdness. For the sons of this world are more shrewd

in dealing with their own generation than the sons of light. (Luke 16:8)

Let's figure out the meaning of the parable. The rich man is HaShem. The wealth manager is you. One thing you need to understand: You don't own anything. Everything you think is yours belongs to God, and he has entrusted it to you to put it to good use for him. We know it's not yours because, before long, God will take it back from you. That's right, you're getting fired. From life.

Until that happens, you need to strategize. There is no way to take it with you. Your best bet is to use what you have now to make friends in the afterlife. Those "friends" are the acts of kindness that you do. Any time you relinquish what you think is yours for someone else's sake—whether that means giving charity, forgiving another person, not demanding what you deserve, or not taking revenge—those credits accrue for you in the World to Come.

Why did Yeshua mention the "sons of light" in that parable? This is a children-of-light story because being a child of light means more than being a good person. It means you are clued into the bigger picture. The perspective of children of darkness can be summarized as, "You only live once." As a child of light, you know that when this life is over, you're just getting started.

BACK TO OUR QUESTIONS

Let's take a moment to revisit the questions we asked earlier.

First, what kind of light is the light of the first day of creation? It is not natural light; it is spiritual light that enables you to understand the purpose of the universe, to know God, and comprehend that there is nothing besides him. You were created because God wanted you to enjoy that light.

Second, in what sense did God separate the light from the darkness? He took this spiritual light and hid it, stashing it away for a time to make space for our own free will. During this life, souls are sifted to separate the children of light from the children of darkness, and only the children of light will get to enjoy the light.

Finally, what is the inheritance of light that Paul talked about? It is the destiny awaiting the righteous when we finally get a glimpse of our creator. As Paul wrote in his letter to the Corinthians:

> For now we see in a mirror dimly, but then face to face. Now I know in part; then I shall know fully, even as I have been fully known. (1 Corinthians 13:12)

MAKING IT REAL

We learned the story of the hidden light and saw how it is worth making it your goal in life to receive that light. That understanding makes life's challenges in this world more bearable and meaningful.

Focusing your eyes on the World to Come doesn't mean losing your grip on day-to-day life. Instead, you gain perspective that will make your immediate circumstances less overwhelming. Decide today that gaining the hidden light is your goal in life. With this perspective, you will have a sense of direction in life. Challenges and stresses will still come, but you will have the right frame of reference to overcome them. Eventually, you will experience the ultimate purpose of your existence: to see from one end of the universe to the other.

Don't stay in a bubble where small things seem big and where your best hope is immediate gratification. In that bubble, you feel stressed by small stuff and frustrated that you can't meet your own standards of spirituality. Instead, become a person on an eternal quest for the hidden light of creation.

STILL IN THE DARK

But we have a problem. The light is hidden. How do we live here and now in the absence of God's light? There must be a way to tap into it. That's what we will learn next.

CHAPTER 2

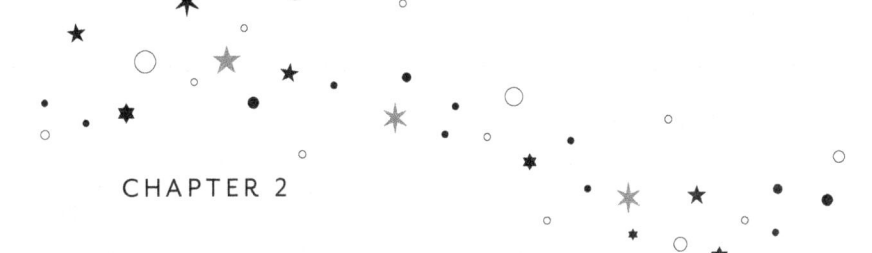

LIGHT OF THE WORLD

Some Christians teach that all humans are inherently wicked from birth and that there is nothing we can do about it. They say we are sinful, depraved, and utterly undeserving of anything from God.

EVIL FROM BIRTH

That idea does not agree with Jewish teaching. In fact, it does not agree with the Bible. The Bible says there are righteous people, people whom God commended and rewarded for their good deeds. To be clear, by "righteous," I don't mean "perfect." We all make mistakes now and then. But in the Bible, someone who makes a few mistakes is not considered a wicked person.

The Torah called Noah a righteous man. The Gospels refer to Yeshua's father, Yosef, as a righteous man. The Psalms and Proverbs often talk about righteous people, how they behave, and how they are rewarded. By the Bible's standards, it is possible to be righteous and rewarded for being righteous, including people who never know about or follow Yeshua. There are people today, including many observant Jews, who live selfless, moral lives; they are dedicated to serving God but do not follow Yeshua. If it is possible to be righteous and receive a reward, what is the advantage of being a disciple of Yeshua?

REACHING FOR THE LIGHT

Let's review what we learned in the last chapter. I told you about the hidden light of creation and that when God said, "Let there be light," it was not light as we know it but a representation of something deeper: the full revelation of God, the universe, and the purpose of life. When God separated it from the darkness, he set it aside, stashing it away for the righteous in the future. Our primary goal is to attain the hidden light as our inheritance in the World to Come.

Having this goal in mind changes the way we live. It means this life is just the entryway, the admission line. Knowing this helps us cope with everyday struggles because we see the bigger picture. It keeps us from being distracted by cheap thrills that are not worth our time. It reminds us to recognize that each moment of free choice is precious and that we should make every second count.

MISSING THE LIGHT

You are on a quest to achieve the hidden light, which is revelation from God. The most important tool you need for your quest is revelation from God to guide you. This is a problem because the existence of wicked people made it necessary for God to hide the light. As a result, God's wisdom and will are not revealed in the world. We lack direction and a sense of God's presence.

It seems unfair for this light to be withheld because of the wicked. Now is precisely when you need the light of God. Your soul's purpose is to bask in the revelation of God. When God's presence is hidden, you feel like something is missing.

THE LIGHTS OF THE WORLD

We're going to find out how to tap into the hidden light. It may be hidden, but it's not hidden very well. God left bread crumbs laced within his universe that point the way for us. He purposely made a way for people who seek him to find him.

When the hidden light is not entirely hidden—when a small sliver of it beams into our current time—what do we call it? The ancient rabbis called it "the light of the world."

THE TORAH

The light of the world broke through in full force with the giving of the Torah at Mount Sinai. The Torah is the revelation of God. It reveals his will and his character. The Torah, in the form of the spoken and written word, is the light of the world.

You can experience the light of the world by reading and hearing, studying, teaching, and doing what the Torah says. If your heart is tuned to it, you will find the hidden light. Proverbs says, "For the commandment (mitzvah) is a lamp and the teaching (the Torah) a light, and the reproofs of discipline are the way of life" (Proverbs 6:23).

The Torah and the rest of the Scriptures are not just a list of dos and don'ts, like a list of chores or rules your parents might give you when they leave the house. It's more like a treasure map, a guide to help you on your quest. As Psalm 119:105 says, "Your word is a lamp to my feet and a light to my path."

If the Torah is the light of the world, then one who teaches the Torah to others is also the light of the world because that person illuminates the path for others.

THE TEMPLE

The Torah is the light of the world in the form of words. But there is a light of the world in physical space: It is Jerusalem, particularly the Temple that is supposed to be there. The Temple was a place where one could physically encounter the presence of God. It was a place that connected heaven and earth. Within the Temple stood the menorah with seven branches holding seven lamps. These seven lights hint at the seven days of creation, during which the hidden light was not yet hidden. In a typical castle with thick stone walls, the windows were built to maximize the amount of light coming in by making the opening larger on the inside. But the windows of the Temple were reversed as if to maximize the amount of light shining out.

You are aligning yourself with the hidden light by directing your heart toward the land of Israel, the city of Jerusalem, and the Temple Mount. The Temple is in ruins, so the light isn't shining brightly like it once did. This is why we pray for God to rebuild it. The Temple is like a lighthouse, a beacon drawing people toward the hidden light of the World to Come.

Isaiah was talking about Jerusalem when he wrote, "For behold, darkness shall cover the earth, and thick darkness the peoples; but the LORD will arise upon you, and his glory will be seen upon you. And nations shall come to your light, and kings to the brightness of your rising" (Isaiah 60:2-3).

SHABBAT

The light of the world also peeks into our universe in the form of time. When you read the story of the creation of the world at the beginning of Genesis, you'll see that each day is marked by the phrase, "and there was evening and there was morning, the first day." "And there was evening and there was morning, the second day." There is one day when it doesn't say that: the seventh day—Shabbat. Why doesn't it say "there was evening" before the first Shabbat?

According to an ancient legend, on the first Shabbat of the universe, there was no darkness because the hidden light illuminated it. The twelve hours of light on the sixth day extended all through Shabbat without ever getting dark.

We often treat Shabbat as a day to relax and recharge so we can get back to the important work we do during the week. But the truth is precisely the opposite. Shabbat is not preparation for the weekdays. The weekdays are preparation for Shabbat. Shabbat is when real life happens. On Shabbat we stop racing against time. We stare it in the face. For twenty-four hours, we simply experience and enjoy time.

Shabbat is a foretaste of the World to Come. It's like when you're in the admission line to the amusement park; as you weave back and forth, there's a spot where you catch a glimpse into the park and see the roller coasters. In this way, Shabbat is a guiding light, leading us to our goal. Doing something every day to prepare for Shabbat, to prepare to experience God, sets your life in order and guides you to the hidden light.

MESSIAH

So far, we've learned that the light of the world comes through the Torah, the Temple, and Shabbat. But there is one more source of the hidden light. This one is the clearest of them all: our Master Yeshua.

Yeshua said this about himself in John 8:12: "I am the light of the world. Whoever follows me will not walk in darkness, but will have the light of life." What makes Yeshua the light of the world? How will those who follow him have light? First, there's the simple answer.

We learned that since Torah is the light of the world, any rabbi or Torah teacher is also the light of the world. Yeshua is our Rabbi. He taught the Torah. In a generation that thought they were Torah-keepers, Yeshua shined the light of Torah and showed where they were falling short. He taught us to focus on the deep intention, the heart of the Torah, not just the technicalities.

Yeshua stunned people with the insightful clarity of his teaching. It was obvious that he was not just another rabbi; he was a prophet. A prophet is someone sent by God with a message. A prophet hears and knows what God wants to say and says it. The people who followed Yeshua could see this. The Gospels teach us that the crowds "were astonished at his teaching, for he taught them as one who had authority, and not as the scribes" (Mark 1:22). Yeshua was tapping into a higher source of revelation; he had prophetic authority. The people also recognized this from his miracles because they knew the stories about the miracles of the prophets like Elijah and Elisha. Mark 6:15 captures their conversation:

> But others said, "He is Elijah." And others said, "He is a prophet, like one of the prophets of old." (Mark 6:15)

While being a prophet is special, there have been many prophets. Isaiah saw visions of heaven. Jeremiah predicted the future and called for repentance. Hosea begged people to embrace the heart of Torah and not just perform meaningless actions. Clearly, Yeshua followed in this vein, but his closest disciples realized that he was more than just one prophet among many:

> [Yeshua] went on with his disciples to the villages of Caesarea Philippi. And on the way he asked his disciples, "Who do people say that I am?" And they told him, "John the Baptist; and others say, Elijah; and others, one of the prophets." And he asked them, "But who do you say that I am?" Peter answered him, "You are the [Messiah]." (Mark 8:27–29)

Now we're talking on a new level. When Peter said "Messiah," he was talking about the promised King. Messiah, or in Hebrew, *Mashiach*, means "anointed," like one anointed to be king. Think of when the Prophet Samuel poured oil on the head of David son of Jesse, designating him as the next king of Israel.

The disciples recognized that they were not merely in the presence of a wise man; they were in the presence of royalty. The greatest King Israel has ever had. A king destined to be a greater conqueror than any emperor in history. When it dawned on the disciples that their rabbi was the Messiah, they understood that the redemption, the culmination point of history and the purpose of the world's existence, would come through him.

The disciples remembered what God had promised King David. In 2 Samuel 7, God promised that the royal line would come through David's children. The prophecy explained that the relationship between God and the king of Israel would be that of father and son. To be the king of Israel means to be the son of God.

If any king of Israel is called the "son of God," then how much more so is the Messiah, the ultimate King. The King who finally rules in peace, victory, righteousness, and godliness. The Messiah embodies what the King of Israel is supposed to be: a perfect representation of God's wisdom and justice on earth, a physical manifestation of God's kingship. Imagine looking at your rabbi, a wandering peasant with dusty clothes, and realizing he is destined to become God's royal representative on earth.

Although they knew this in their hearts that day in Caesarea Philippi, it must have been hard to wrap their minds around it. Until one week later. Yeshua took three of his disciples, Shimon, Ya'akov, and Yochanan, up on a mountain, and they caught a glimpse of his true identity:

> He was transfigured [his appearance was transformed] before them, and his face shone like the sun, and his clothes became white as light. And behold, there appeared to them Moses and Elijah, talking with him. And Peter said to [Yeshua], "Lord, it is good that we are here. If you wish, I will make three tents here, one for you and one for Moses and one for Elijah." He was still speak-

ing when, behold, a bright cloud overshadowed them, and a voice from the cloud said, "This is my beloved Son, with whom I am well pleased; listen to him." When the disciples heard this, they fell on their faces and were terrified. (Matthew 17:2-6)

Can you imagine having this experience? Any doubts that those three disciples had before evaporated. It was clear that their rabbi was unlike any other.

Their minds must have been racing with ideas. Maybe they thought about the psalms that describe Messiah being greater than King David and a priest in the line of Melchizedek (Psalm 110). Or the prophecies that say that the Messiah's origins are from ages past and that the Spirit of God fills him. The *midrashim*, the legends, say that the Messiah's name existed before creation and that the Spirit of God that hovered over the water of creation was the Spirit of Messiah.

Not long afterward, Yeshua was arrested and charged with insurrection. They saw him brutally executed and buried. Stunned and crushed, they mourned together. Then he was alive again, and apparently, he had crazy superpowers like the ability to teleport. They thought his teachings were profound before; now, the mysteries he revealed were blowing their minds. A few weeks later, they watched him rocket into the sky. This was no longer a typical rabbi-student experience.

They shared their stories and insights with each other, they collected testimony and history, and they drew some amazing conclusions. Yes, Yeshua was a real human who was born and lived a regular life. He had a mom and dad and brothers and a job, ate food, went to the bathroom, got hurt sometimes, and felt emotions. But there was something about his soul that came from beyond. Something about him that could be described only in mystical terms. When God spoke the world into being, saying the words "Let there be light"—the speech emerging from God's mouth that turned nothing into something—that speech was, in some sense, Messiah himself. The beam of light that fired into the empty hollow of space and began to 3D print the universe was the Messiah. There is an aspect of Yeshua's identity that transcends creation to the point where *ein od milvado*—there is nothing apart from God—is a conscious reality.

This is what the Gospel of John is teaching us in the first chapter:

> In the beginning was the Word, and the Word was with God, and the Word was God. He was in the beginning with God. All things were made through him, and without him was not any thing made that was made. In him was life, and the life was the light of men. The light shines in the darkness, and the darkness has not overcome it. (John 1:1–5)

Talk about the light of the world! If you want to experience the light of the world now and not wait until the World to Come, you must bind yourself to Yeshua.

BIND YOURSELF TO HIM

In John 12, Yeshua said,

> The light is among you for a little while longer. Walk while you have the light, lest darkness overtake you. The one who walks in the darkness does not know where he is going. While you have the light, believe in the light, that you may become sons of light [i.e., children of light]. (John 12:35–36)

What does he mean by "believe in the light"? In the Gospel of John, "believing" in Yeshua is not just agreeing that he's real, like believing in Santa Claus. It means listening to his teaching, accepting it, and acting on it. Yeshua assures us that he is the light—he is the guide who will bring us from this world where God is hidden into the perfect state of existence where God is revealed. He shows us how to receive the hidden light as our inheritance, making us children of light.

Binding ourselves to Yeshua means becoming his disciple. Being a disciple has some perks. First, you gain access to Yeshua's merit and connection to God. God no longer sees you as someone struggling to be a good person. Now you are a mini-Messiah, and when he sees you, he says, "This is my beloved child, with whom I am well pleased."

As a mini-Messiah, you have a job to do in this world. Sometimes, you won't have the necessary tools and resources to accomplish the job. But as a disciple, you have the right to ask for what you need. You can say to God, "To carry out my duties as a disciple of Yeshua, here are the things I need." Maybe you need wisdom, joy, health, or a better job.

In fact, Yeshua gives us access to *Ruach HaKodesh*, the divine Spirit. In the Messianic Era, this gift will be poured out on everyone, but as a disciple of Yeshua, you have the exclusive right to ask for it now.

As a mini-Messiah, it is your privilege to partner with Yeshua in the redemption of the world. Your job is to bring the world to its purpose for existing.

Another benefit is that as a disciple, you will have a share in the resurrection of the righteous. That is something you won't want to miss.

BECOMING A DISCIPLE

Being a disciple is not automatic. It is not inherited. Becoming a disciple does not mean identifying with a religious group, joining a denomination, or attending a congregation.

When you become a disciple of Yeshua, you enroll as a lifetime student in a school. To become Yeshua's disciple, you must personally decide to devote yourself to him. Becoming a disciple and enrolling in his school means you are embarking on a new relationship with God and with Yeshua and forming a bond with all other disciples.

Many Christians make a big deal about praying the "sinner's prayer," asking Jesus to come into your heart. That's not a bad thing to do, but the Bible doesn't say anywhere that you need to do that or that it makes you a disciple. The Bible does say that you need to confess your sins and repent and rely on God's mercy, which you will continue to do even after you are a disciple.

According to the New Testament, the most important outward step in becoming a disciple is getting immersed in water. You can use a lake or a river, an ocean or a mikvah. It doesn't really matter. At this initiation ceremony, there should be witnesses to hear you express your faith and devotion to Yeshua and who welcome you into the school of disciples.

Is it possible to be a disciple without being immersed? I guess, probably. But immersion is not an optional step, and there is no good reason not to. In the first century, you likely would not have been treated as a disciple in the community until you were immersed. If you already consider yourself a disciple or would like to become a disciple, and have not yet been immersed, don't wait. Find some other disciples and ask them to help you get immersed.

I can't emphasize this enough. Becoming immersed as a disciple is not optional. It is the normal procedure for becoming a disciple of Yeshua. Make it happen as soon as you know that's who you are. Once you are initiated into this school, you embark on your education. You learn his words, his ways, and his teachings, and you imitate him. You identify with him and become his agent in the world.

To a disciple, the words of Yeshua are like precious jewels you collect by memorizing them. You spend time every day reading those words, trying to understand them, and trying to engrave them in your mind. You live a life of intention, carefully trying to make your behavior match the principles your master lived and taught. It's a lifelong process.

In so doing, you experience the divine light, the hidden light. Your path is illuminated, and you are becoming a child of light. You are helping to bring the world closer to redemption one step at a time.

THE POINT OF DISCIPLESHIP

At the beginning of this chapter, I asked the question, "If it is possible to be righteous and receive a reward, then what is the advantage of being a disciple of Yeshua?" The answer should now be clear. There is more to life than trying to be good; we are on a mission to redeem the world, to bring it to the purpose for which it was created.

Yeshua is more than a wise man or a rabbi; he is the clearest distillation of the hidden light available to us. His teachings are what will bring humanity to its fulfillment. Being his disciple gives your life purpose right now and grants incredible benefits for the future.

You are on a quest to achieve the hidden light and get revelation from God. How can you get this revelation without some guidance in the meantime?

We learned how to access the hidden light even now. The Torah, the Temple, and Shabbat are all lights that guide our way. Our Master Yeshua is the living Torah. Like the Temple, he is filled with the presence of God. Just as Shabbat gives us a taste of the Messianic Era, Yeshua, the Messiah in our midst, helps us experience the Messianic Kingdom right now.

I want to challenge you to commit yourself now as a disciple of Yeshua. Not just someone who hangs out in Messianic circles. Make discipleship your primary identity above anything else that describes you.

If you have not yet been immersed, make it happen. Ask your parents or congregational leaders to help you with this; if they don't act on it right away, pester them. If you're not ready for immersion, learn more about Yeshua and what he taught.

It won't happen all at once, but as you progress further down the path of discipleship, you will gain more clarity and insight. At dawn, the sky is still dark, but you start to see sunlight glowing in the east. Dawn light is dim light, but it increases. Proverbs says, "But the path of the righteous is like the light of dawn, which shines brighter and brighter until full day" (Proverbs 4:18). The "full day" is the ultimate redemption when we receive our inheritance as children of light.

As you set yourself on this dim but brightening path, you will no longer just be a person in a weird religious group; you'll be plugged into the source of the universe—the unknowable God—through the Messiah. You'll be able to reveal this hidden light to the world.

NORMAL HUMAN

But there is still a problem. You'll never stop being a normal human with weaknesses and failures. How do you reveal this hidden light to others without it becoming an act? That's what we will discuss next.

CHAPTER 3

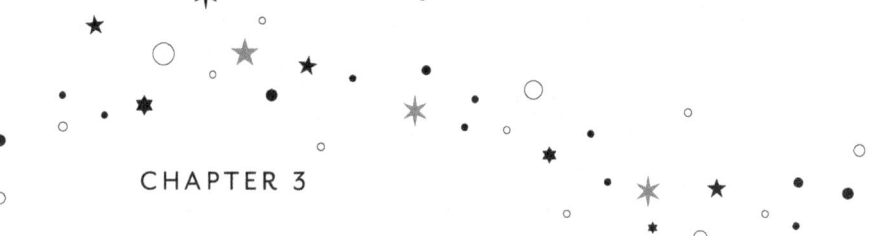

The Light Within

Imagine you were hired to be in God's marketing company. Let's say he wanted you to design a billboard to advertise him to the world. What would you put on it? How would you show the world who he is?

TO BE SEEN BY MEN

The Sermon on the Mount is Yeshua's central set of teachings. It's recorded in Matthew chapters 5, 6, and 7. If you're a disciple, it's important that you learn it well, even memorize it. But if you look at it carefully, you'll notice a strange, blatant contradiction.

In Matthew 6:1, Yeshua said, "Beware of practicing your righteousness before other people in order to be seen by them, for then you will have no reward from your Father who is in heaven."

But only a few paragraphs earlier, in Matthew 5:16, Yeshua said, "In the same way, let your light shine before others, so that they may see your good works and give glory to your Father who is in heaven."

Which is it? Are we supposed to do righteous deeds in secret, or should we do our righteous acts publicly so that others see us?

MINI-MESSIAH

In the last chapter we talked about a different contradiction. We're supposed to seek the light of creation, the full revelation of God and his universe. But God hid it from us until the World to Come. This is good because it gives us room for free will. But it also creates a challenge.

Without revelation from God, how is there any chance that we will find the hidden light? We need the hidden light to find the hidden light.

Fortunately, the hidden light is not entirely hidden. It beams into our world enough for someone to find it if he or she truly seeks it. It's the Torah, the Temple, Shabbat, and most of all, the Messiah Yeshua.

The best way to ensure that you are a child of light, destined to receive the hidden light, is to devote yourself entirely to Yeshua, to become his disciple and his agent in this world. One step that you cannot skip is getting immersed. When you do this, you commit yourself not only to Yeshua but to the whole community of his disciples.

Now that you are a disciple, you are progressing toward the full light of God's revelation. You have become a mini-Messiah yourself, an agent of redemption in the world, and a light revealing godliness to the world.

RELIGIOUS ACT

This journey presents you with a difficulty. As a disciple with the light of Messiah in you, you want to make a difference in the world. The problem is you. You're a normal person. You're not a divine being or an angel. And everywhere you go, there you are. Maybe you hoped that you would magically become super holy by getting immersed as a disciple. But you don't feel much different from everyone else. You're not capable of revealing divine light.

You decide, "Okay, I will at least do my best." But when you try to be spiritual, you appear to think you're better than everyone else, or you're showing off how holy and religious and spiritual you are. You come across to people as "holier than thou" or hypocritical. You seem like you're trying to get attention for being more religious, and nobody likes that. It backfires.

If living a religious life makes people less interested in God, then what's the point? So, you tone down the religious stuff and just try to fit in. But then you feel even more hypocritical because now you're acting in a way that doesn't reflect your beliefs.

As a disciple, an agent of God in the world, you should be able to reveal godliness in a way that appeals to others. It shouldn't make you seem like a phony. All religious people deal with this problem, especially people in leadership. Here's the question: How can we reveal the light of Messiah in an authentic, naturally appealing way?

We will discuss one key attribute that will make your faith more attractive to others. More importantly, it will make your faith true to yourself, and you can authentically represent Yeshua.

GRASPING EQUALITY WITH GOD

Let's think about the story of the garden of Eden. I assume you know the story, so I won't go into detail. In a nutshell, God created Adam and Eve. We learn that God created humans in his image, in a way that resembles him. He instructed them to take care of the garden and warned them not to eat the fruit from a particular tree: the tree of the knowledge of good and evil.

The snake came along and tried to convince them to eat this fruit, explaining that they would become like God, knowing good and evil if they did. The woman saw that the fruit was good for food, and she took it and ate it.

This raises some questions:

- ★ Adam and Eve were already like God; after all, he made them in his image. In what way could they become like God?
- ★ God is the one who defines good and evil. Obeying him is good; disobeying him is evil. So they already knew good and evil. What more knowledge could they gain?
- ★ When Eve looked at the fruit, she saw that it was good for food. How could she tell it was good if eating the fruit was the only way for her to know what was "good"?

IMITATING THE MASTER

With these questions in mind, let's look at a passage that might be less familiar. This teaching explains the importance of humility. Our Master Yeshua excelled at humility, and here we learn how important it is to imitate him in this way:

> Do nothing from rivalry or conceit, but in humility count others more significant than yourselves. Let each of you look not only to his own interests, but also to the interests of others. (Philippians 2:3-4)

Let me try rewording this:

> Don't do anything just to advance your own status or make yourself look good. Instead, treat all other people as more important than yourself. Do not think about only your own wants and needs but also be concerned about what others want and need.

Let's look at the next verse:

> Have this mind among yourselves, which is yours in
> [Messiah Yeshua]. (Philippians 2:5)

In other words, let us all have the same way of thinking that Yeshua the Messiah had, "who, though he was in the form of God, did not count equality with God a thing to be grasped."

This is a reference to the garden of Eden. Adam and Eve were made in the image of God. The serpent claimed that if they ate the fruit, they would become equal with God, not just like God.

Good and bad both depend on the purpose. For example, you might have a cardboard box that is good for storing shoes but bad for storing gasoline. The only way to judge something as "good" or "bad" is to compare it to a purpose or plan. When someone asks you, "Is this good?" You have to figure out, "good for what?"

What about things that are definitely bad, like murder, or good, like kindness? Those are what we call moral absolutes. Objective good and evil. But to know that these are good and bad, we still compare each of them to a purpose. We compare them to God's purpose. Murder is opposed to God's purposes, so it's objectively bad. Kindness serves God's purpose, so it's objectively good. For Adam and Eve to decide on their own whether something was good or bad, they had to form their own purpose separate from God's. Having their separate purpose, their own plan, was what would make them not only in the image of God but seeking equality with him.

Adam and Eve were not content being in the image of God and having God tell them what to do. Instead, they wanted to be equal to God and set their own course as they saw fit. The fruit did not have a magical ability to open their eyes to good and evil. It was the act of choosing it, deciding for themselves that it was good. They replaced God's purpose with their own purpose. The moment Eve decided for herself that the fruit was good for food, she had already developed her own purpose and imagined herself as equal to God.

Yeshua, like Adam and Eve, was created in the image of God. But Yeshua forfeited any right to set the course for his own life. Instead, he accepted God's instructions for him:

> Who, though he was in the form of God, did not count equality with God a thing to be grasped, but emptied himself, by taking the form of a servant, being born in the likeness of men. (Philippians 2:6-7)

Unlike Adam and Eve, who greedily stuffed their mouths with the forbidden fruit, Yeshua emptied himself. He denied the right to decide his own mission in life. Instead, he became a servant:

> Being found in human form, he humbled himself by becoming obedient to the point of death, even death on a cross. (Philippians 2:8)

In other words, Yeshua so completely let go of his own agenda that he willingly gave up his life and was tortured to death to do what God asked of him—what God said was "good":

> Therefore God has highly exalted him and bestowed on him the name that is above every name, so that at the name of [Yeshua] every knee should bow, in heaven and on earth and under the earth, and every tongue confess that [Yeshua the Messiah] is Lord, to the glory of God the Father. (Philippians 2:9-11)

"Therefore" means "That is the reason why." Why did God exalt Yeshua? Why did he give him the highest authority on earth? It is because he was humble, and in his humility, he nullified himself. He made himself like nothing.

Yeshua is our example of humility, the character trait that will make our faith authentic. Let's talk about true humility because it sometimes gets confused with other things, like low self-esteem.

Humility is mentioned all over the Bible. According to the greatest minds in Judaism, humility is the starting point for the service of God. Without humility, you can't get anywhere in your walk with God.

HUMILITY AND PURPOSE

Humility is the awareness of your own nothingness. You don't have a reason to exist. God has a reason for you to exist. Being born was not your decision. You exist only because God has a purpose and decided to involve you in it. You have no purpose outside of that. Because you have no purpose, you have no needs. To need something, you must have a purpose. For example, you might say, "I need flour to make a cake," but without a purpose such as baking, you don't need flour.

If you don't have a reason to exist, you don't need to eat or breathe; you don't even need to live. Only God needs you to eat, breathe, and live because he is the one with a purpose, and you are part of his purpose. You are the flour in his cake. Humility means acknowledging this truth about yourself: As a self, you are nothing. Imagining yourself to be something is the same as Adam and Eve grasping at equality with God. Only God is something. Your existence serves only to accomplish God's purpose.

Humility means knowing that you deserve nothing. You can take credit for nothing. Can't you take credit for the things you worked hard to achieve? Let's break that down. You worked hard because you have decent health. Because you are intelligent. That health and intelligence came from your genetics, your environment, how you were nourished, how you were educated, and your opportunities. You can't take credit for any of those things.

Do you think you worked hard because you have a strong work ethic? Who gave you that strong work ethic, that resolve and perseverance? Where did you learn that? You worked hard because you had opportunities given to you. There is nothing you have, including your accomplishments, your gifts, your talents, your strengths, your intelligence, your health, and the money in your pocket that comes from you. All of it was given to you from above. It could all be taken from you instantly, and you would have nothing to say about it.

All these are gifts from above; acknowledge and celebrate them, use them, and be thankful for them. But don't take credit for them. You can claim credit for only one thing: your moral choices—your decision to choose right or wrong. To choose God's purpose or your own purpose. That choice belongs to you and no one else.

Humility is the opposite of pride. Pride is when you ascribe to yourself independent importance. When you imagine yourself to be capable of achievement and deserving of honor, that's pride. Pride is hyper-consciousness of self.

You might think, then, that humility means low self-esteem or self-denigration. When you have a bad self-image and think of yourself as horrible or stupid, that's not humility. Being timid, embarrassed, and shy is not humility. Like pride, these things are also the opposite of humility. Remember, humility is awareness of your own nothingness. When you think of yourself so negatively, you give yourself way too much focus. Do you think you're ugly? What do you have to do with it? You didn't make your face. You didn't choose your body. God's opinion is all that matters.

Pride and arrogance are often masks for insecurity and low self-esteem. Both come from being self-focused. You cannot be consumed with self-consciousness and also humble. Humility replaces self-consciousness with God-consciousness.

WHAT HUMILITY LOOKS LIKE

What is a humble person like? Humble people speak gently. They don't feel a need to attract attention or be provocative. They don't demand an audience. They don't demand honor for themselves. They don't put other people down or even put them in their place. They speak with dignity to everyone.

Humble people don't have a bad temper. They never take revenge. They forgive easily because they lack ego. They are not bothered when someone insults them or humiliates them. They certainly don't retaliate or hurl insults back. A humble person doesn't worry about clever comebacks.

We all experience loss in our lives. Humble people accept when God takes things away because they don't feel entitled to anything. When their plans fall through, it doesn't unsettle them because they know God is the one with the real plan.

Humble people don't try to hang out with the in-crowd. Yeshua taught that if you are invited to a formal banquet where guests are seated in order of rank, you should sit at the lowest spot at the table. Nowadays, dinner guests are not often arranged by rank, but you might notice people do this instinctively. What is it like at your school? Do people with high popularity or social rank sit together at lunch? A humble person finds the people with the lowest social rank and sits with them.

Humble people love criticism. They love to learn, even from people who are not as smart as them. When they learn something, they say, "Thank you for teaching me." When they don't know the answer to a question, they say, "I don't know." When someone notices something good they've done, they don't let it go to their heads. They recognize where that accomplishment came from and acknowledge how much they have yet to accomplish.

When someone points out that a humble person has done something wrong, the humble person doesn't attempt to justify himself. He doesn't blame it on someone else or deflect. He doesn't try to discredit the person accusing him. Instead, he takes responsibility and faces the consequences. Even false accusations, a humble person takes them in stride. He stands up for the truth but doesn't react with hate.

When humble people realize they have hurt someone else, they will apologize and seek reconciliation even if no one asked them to do this. They have nothing to gain from it, even if they could easily walk away and never face a consequence.

Humble people never look at a task as being "beneath" them. They would never say, "I've paid my dues, so I don't ever have to do that anymore." Or, "Why should I have to do that?" Instead, they are constantly looking for ways to help and serve others, even in boring and simple ways, even if they never get acknowledged for it.

Humble people express humility in their body language. They stand and walk in a posture that shows acceptance and accessibility. They smile at others. They acknowledge when other people are around. They greet other people, including people who are not well-liked. Humble people try to be the first to say "hello" to everyone.

Humble people are not overly preoccupied with fashion or aesthetics. They don't obsess over luxuries and entertainment.

Even though they don't seek the spotlight, humble people are not timid when it's necessary to take action and show leadership. Humble people have a healthy sense of shame that keeps them from doing stupid or inappropriate things, even when no one is looking. But they are not embarrassed to do what's right because they aren't self-conscious. They know that they are nothing but servants.

SELF-NULLIFICATION

Remember, our goal is to reveal the divine light. We cling to Yeshua and the Torah because those are sources of the hidden light in this world. But the harder we try to share that light with the world, the more we can look disingenuous and fake. The reason for this is that we neglect one foundational step: self-nullification. Nullification means making something into nothing. Humility is an awareness that, in reality, you are nothing. Self-nullification is what that awareness looks like in practice.

There was once a king who purchased a palace on a mountainside. The dining room of this palace had an enormous window, but it was boarded up with ugly planks. The king hired a great artisan known for his gorgeous stained-glass windows and told him to install a beautiful window in that room and to spare no expense. The artisan crafted an exquisite stained-glass window with stunning colors and elegant shapes. But the king was not happy with it, so he hired a second craftsman. This artisan constructed an elaborate stained-glass masterpiece depicting plants, animals, and angelic beings, gleaming with bright colors and glinting with gold and precious jewels. When the king saw it, he said, "This is a lovely window." But he still was unsatisfied and decided to hire one more craftsman, the greatest in all the land. When the third craftsman began taking down the old window and saw the breathtaking view of the valley, he said, "There is no way I can compete with this beauty!" So he installed a single sheet of transparent glass. When the king walked in, the window was invisible; all he saw was the magnificent valley. "This is the beauty I was hoping to find," said the king.

This is our problem. When we think of ourselves as God's marketing company—the people who design his ads—we will fail. Any billboard we try to design for God will make him look small and shallow compared to who he really is. Our goal is not to make God look good. God is good. Our real goal is to make ourselves invisible, so God's beauty shines through. To do this, we must practice self-nullification. This means becoming nothing.

A prophet is someone who represents God to the world. There is no such thing as a "great" prophet because the clearer and better a person's prophecy, the more humble and invisible that person will be. The greatest prophet is the one who becomes insignificant. It is no coincidence that Moses, the father of the prophets, who spoke with God face to face, was also the humblest man in the world.

Let's go back to the question I asked at the beginning of the chapter. In Matthew 6:1, Yeshua said, "Beware of practicing your righteousness before other people in order to be seen by them, for then you will have no reward from your Father who is in heaven." In Matthew 5:16, Yeshua said, "In the same way, let your light shine before others, so that they may see your good works and give glory to your Father who is in heaven."

Which is it? Are we supposed to do righteous deeds in secret so that other people don't see us, or should we do our righteous acts so that others see us?

The difference is self-nullification. Are you a stained-glass window or a transparent pane of glass? We must not practice good deeds so that *we* can be seen by others. This is showmanship. It is fake and unattractive. It is also worthless to God.

Yeshua told us that we must let our light shine before others. We must be utterly invisible through humility and self-nullification, letting the hidden light pass through us. So that they see us? No, so they may see *our good works* because that is the hidden light in action. Ideally, they should see our good works and then completely ignore us. When done in humility, the works will cause them to give all the credit to God; only then will we have done our duty.

This will appeal more to others because it will be authentic and genuine. Nonetheless, most people will still reject it. That's the way free will works. But if you are accurately shining the light of the world, their acceptance or rejection of it is not your problem.

INVISIBLE

Do you exist to be the image of God, or do you exist to seek equality with God? The choice is yours, and it depends on whether you have submitted yourself to God's purpose or pursued your own purpose. The key to authentic faith is to imitate Yeshua. If anyone on earth deserved to take credit for themselves or to pursue his own ambitions, it was Yeshua. And yet he said, "Not as I will, but as you will" (Matthew 26:39).

Take the next twenty-four hours to focus on becoming a humble person. Do some small, selfless act today. Do something to help another person. Try to do it in such a way that you won't get credit or even a thank-you. If you do happen to get noticed, that's okay. As long as you weren't seeking it, you accomplished your mission.

If you develop this trait of humility, you won't be God's PR agent anymore. You won't have to make him look cool. You will become invisible, and if God doesn't look cool enough for this world, then that's his problem to fix, not yours.

Becoming nothing is difficult. It's a sacrifice few people are willing to make. We all crave attention and credit. But if you give up, eventually, acting like a religious person will wear on you, and you won't be able to maintain the illusion for very long.

By nullifying yourself, you won't have to feel like a showy religious person, timid about your faith, or hypocritical. You are a child of light. As children of light, you reveal God's light in the world.

DARKNESS CREEPS IN

This world is dark, and it's getting darker. Darkness does not like light; it wants to extinguish it. How do you keep the godless culture from eating away at your purity and compromising your holiness? How is it possible to shine the light of God in such a dark world? This is what we will discuss next.

CHAPTER 4

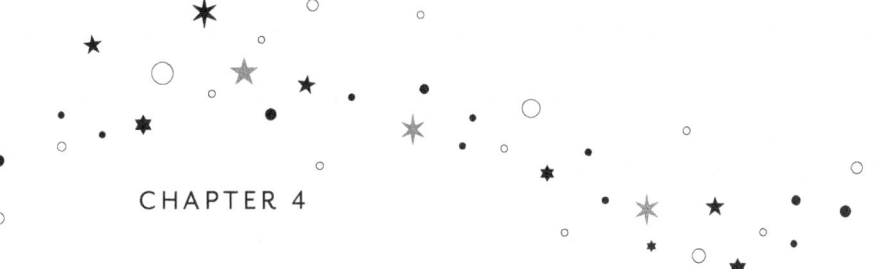

Separating from the Darkness

In the last chapter, we discussed the challenge of being a light to the world without looking like a hypocrite. We learned that the key to success is getting yourself out of the way. Instead of attempting to stand in for God, let God represent himself. He does a better job than we do. You need to practice humility and self-nullification to get yourself out of the way.

TRANSPARENT

When we think about Adam and Eve, we might wonder why they couldn't follow simple instructions. We imagine that in their place, we would have followed God's instructions and not ended up in this mess.

We need to understand that the real temptation of Adam and Eve was not a piece of fruit; the temptation was to choose their own purpose in life. "Good" and "bad" have meaning only when compared to a purpose. By eating from the tree of the knowledge of good and evil, they decided that being in the image of God wasn't good enough; they wanted to be equal to God. God has a purpose and plan for the universe. Adam and Eve wanted to be like God and assert their own purpose and plan.

The Apostle Paul encouraged us to have the same mindset as Yeshua. If you think you would not have made Adam and Eve's mistake, compare your own life and decisions to Yeshua's.

Even though he was in the image of God, he did not try to achieve equality with God by setting his own course for his life. Instead of filling himself, he emptied himself. He nullified himself and his plans, to the point of allowing himself to be tortured to death. This humility is why God set Yeshua in a place of ultimate authority.

Paul teaches us to follow Yeshua, be humble, nullify ourselves, and treat everyone else as more important. Humility is the awareness that you are nothing. The act of self-nullification is turning that awareness into a concrete reality. If we do this, and I think we can, we will channel the hidden light into our world.

IT'S DARK OUT THERE

Now we encounter a new difficulty. You have nullified yourself. You have the light of the Messiah, the light of the world within you. You want to shine it into the world and reveal godliness to everyone. The problem is that the darkness is overwhelming; it wants to extinguish the light. The light threatens the darkness; after all, light exposes darkness. The godless culture eats away at your purity, compromising your holiness.

The darkness is all around you. It's coming from school, the internet, TV and movies, and music. It's companies trying to sell you products. It's games; it's politics. It's coming from your co-workers, neighbors, relatives, and friends. The pressure to compromise is coming from the entire civilization around you. There is no getting away from it, and even if you could get away, that would defeat the purpose of being a light to the world.

The darkness is affecting you. You do things, you think things, you see things, and you joke about things that you know you shouldn't. You spend more time than you ought to be distracted by entertainment and media rather than fulfilling your purpose in life. You feel guilty about it sometimes, but that doesn't stop you. The darkness continues to draw you in.

We are told that a little light dispels a lot of darkness. That's true. But in our world, the overwhelming darkness of society is smothering the light. Many people initially have pure intentions but can't maintain their spiritual strength and eventually give in to the surrounding culture. This is not a new problem. The people of God have faced this challenge in every generation. How do we stand firm as children of light and keep from being overwhelmed by the darkness of the world around us?

In this chapter we will find guidance in the story of a people surrounded by one of the darkest cultures in history. We find the story in the Torah in Parashat Va'era (Exodus 6:2–9:35). We will see the hidden pattern in the plagues of Egypt and the message behind the Passover lamb. We will discuss some practical strategies for standing strong and shining God's light in a dark world.

THE TEN PLAGUES

In this story, God tells Moses that he has heard the groaning of the Israelites under Egyptian slavery, and he promises that he is about to take them out of Egypt with great acts of judgment.

At God's instruction, Moses and Aaron went to Pharaoh and told him to let the people go. To show God's power, Aaron threw down his staff, and it became a snake. Pharaoh's magicians also turned their staffs into snakes. Even though Aaron's staff ate all their staffs, Pharaoh's heart remained hard, and he would not let the people go. So let the ten plagues commence! Blood, frogs, lice, swarms (of wild animals), livestock disease, boils, hail, locusts, darkness, and the death of the firstborn.

At first, the choice of plagues seems a little random. If I wrote the story, this is not the list of natural disasters I would have chosen. But we'll see the pattern and find out what it can teach us about our lives. The ten plagues were a judgment against the gods of Egypt, each one climbing up the hierarchy of false gods. To us, it seems random, but to the Egyptians and the Israelites, the message of each plague was clear.

The pattern gets even more interesting. To see it, you have to read the text carefully. Before the first plague—blood—Pharaoh was warned that it was about to happen. God told Moses to stand by the Nile River in the morning and wait there for Pharaoh. Before the plague of frogs, Pharaoh was also warned, but this time, God told Moses to walk right into Pharaoh's palace. Then, before the plague of lice, Pharaoh got no warning at all.

We see something similar with the following three plagues. Before the swarms, Pharaoh was warned, and like with the first plague, God told Moses to stand by the Nile and wait for him. Before the plague of livestock disease, Pharaoh was warned again, but this time God told Moses to walk into Pharaoh's palace again. Then, before the sixth plague, the plague of boils, Pharaoh got no warning at all.

The pattern repeats a third time; Moses encroached on Pharaoh's domain more with each plague. Before the hail, Pharaoh was warned by Moses, who waited for him by the Nile in the morning. Then there were locusts. Pharaoh was warned when Moses walked into his palace. For the ninth plague, darkness, there was no warning.

The plagues came in three waves of three. The tenth plague, the death of the firstborn, hit Egypt with no warning.

What was the meaning of these three waves? God explains each one. The first time Moses and Aaron came to Pharaoh to tell him to let the people go, Pharaoh refused. This is how Pharaoh answered:

> Pharaoh said, "Who is the LORD, that I should obey his voice and let Israel go? I do not know the LORD, and moreover, I will not let Israel go." (Exodus 5:2)

Pharaoh didn't know God. The plagues came to solve his problem. Before the first set of three plagues, God explained to Moses, "By this you shall know that I am the LORD" (Exodus 7:17). The plagues of blood, frogs, and lice proved to Pharaoh that HaShem was real.

But Pharaoh might still think that HaShem is a distant god of nature who sends natural disasters occasionally but does not take sides in human affairs. So before the second set of plagues, God gave Moses a new explanation: "That you may know that I am the LORD in the midst of the earth" (Exodus 8:18[22]). In other words, "I'm involved."

The second set of plagues was different from the first in another way. They struck only the Egyptians, not the Israelites. Notice what God said before the fourth plague, swarms: "But on that day I will set apart the land of Goshen, where my people dwell" (Exodus 8:18[22]). Before the fifth plague, the livestock, it says, "But the LORD will make a distinction between the livestock of Israel and the livestock of Egypt, so that nothing of all that belongs to the people of Israel shall die" (Exodus 9:4). The sixth, the plague of boils, also affected only the Egyptians.

In the second wave of plagues, God separated the Israelites from the Egyptians, claiming them as his own people. This showed Pharaoh that HaShem was not a distant god of nature. He takes sides in human affairs.

Now Pharaoh knows that HaShem is the God of Israel. But the tribal deity of the Israelites surely cannot compete with the power of the Egyptian pantheon! Pharaoh has a new lesson to learn with the final wave.

Before the plague of hail, God said, "But for this purpose I have raised you up, to show you my power, so that my name may be proclaimed in all the earth" (Exodus 9:16). Moses called the locust invasion something that "neither your fathers nor your grandfathers have seen, from the day they came on earth to this day" (Exodus 10:6). The plague of darkness was not normal darkness; it was unnatural darkness that the Egyptians could feel. These three plagues showed Pharaoh that God's power was limitless.

THE PASSOVER LAMB

This brings us to the tenth plague—the death of the firstborn. God orchestrated this plague from the start. Back when Moses was in Midian, God said, "Israel is my firstborn son ... If you refuse to let him go, behold, I will kill your firstborn son" (Exodus 4:22-23). The final plague was unique. Like the others, it was a judgment against a god of Egypt; it proved that HaShem exists, that he is all-powerful, and that Israel is his people. But unlike the other nine plagues, it required the Jewish people to take decisive action. They couldn't sit back and watch the events unfold.

This was when Israel received their first *mitzvot*, their first commandments, as a nation. On the tenth of the month, they were to select an unblemished lamb or goat less than one year old, one for each household. A small family would share with their neighbors. After four days, they would slaughter it, paint its blood on their door frame, roast it, and eat it with matzah and bitter herbs. As God passed through to strike the Egyptians, he would not let the destroyer into the homes marked with blood on the door frame.

Previously, God spared the Israelites without any action on their part. Why are they suddenly required to perform this lamb ceremony? The sacrifice of a lamb or goat was incredibly offensive to the Egyptians. The oldest of the Egyptian gods was a ram god named Khnum. They called him the "father of fathers." They considered him the ancestor of Ra and the creator of the Nile. They imagined him as a potter who formed children in their mothers' wombs.

Earlier in the story, Pharaoh had offered to let the Israelites make sacrifices inside the land of Egypt. Moses objected, saying, "It would not be right to do so, for the offerings we shall sacrifice to the LORD our God are an abomination to the Egyptians. If we sacrifice offerings abominable to the Egyptians before their eyes, will they not stone us?" (Exodus 8:26) But that was precisely what they were doing. The Passover lamb sacrifice was an abomination; in other words, it was terribly offensive to the Egyptians.

The way they did the Passover offering in Egypt was special and never to be repeated. All other sacrifices were offered only in the Tabernacle or the Temple; the blood was applied to an altar; only the priests offered and ate them. But with the first Passover lamb, every family was a priesthood, every house was a sanctuary, and every door frame was an altar. All this happened in the darkest and most impure place on earth.

The Passover lamb required the Israelites to take a stand. They defied the Egyptian gods to their faces. They held onto a lamb for four days while the Egyptians looked on in disgust. They had to rely on and coordinate with one another. Their homes became sacred places, a physical boundary that separated them from the Egyptians and united them with their own people.

Before, they might have thought, "Are we really that different from the Egyptians?" But the Passover lamb came to tell them that they were completely different. They were from a different world.

God had already singled them out, demonstrating his exclusive loyalty to Israel. With the Passover lamb, it was their turn to own that unique identity, to separate themselves.

MAKING A DISTINCTION

This is the answer to our problem. You must do three things to maintain your integrity as a disciple of Yeshua in this world and keep your light from being overwhelmed by the darkness.

First, unite with godly peers. Connect with other disciples who will strengthen and support you. Second, keep your worldly friends at arm's length. And third, be different from the surrounding culture. Let's take a closer look at each of these strategies.

CONNECT

The Passover lamb required each person to unite with a household and family, to gather under the same roof. To keep your light shining, you need to connect with other disciples who will support and strengthen you. It's like logs in a campfire. When they are together, they burn brightly. But if you separate and scatter them, the fire dies.

Judaism is a communal religion, not a monastic one. This means that it is not just about your personal relationship with God. That's important, of course, but biblical faith is also about your relationship with a community, with a people, and with history.

The New Testament calls our community a body. You are only a part. You are not meant to live on your own. To properly grow in faith and holiness, you need three things: teachers, peers, and students.

Who are your teachers? Who are you accountable to? If you don't have a spiritual mentor, you've got to find one or more. Seek out people whom you respect and trust.

Who are your peers? As much as you learn and are strengthened by mentors, you will learn and be strengthened even more by godly peers. Who do you study and pray with? The Jewish community has learned over thousands of years that the best study method is called a *chavruta*. This is a partner study in which you tackle a topic together, ask each other questions, and challenge and debate each other to understand and learn.

Who are your students? As much as you learn and are strengthened by your partners and your mentors, you will learn and be strengthened even more by your students. Who are you mentoring? It doesn't have to be a formal relationship, but you should be looking for people who need guidance and encouragement and helping them in any way you can.

As a disciple of Yeshua, being a member of this body is the most critical part of your identity. It's more significant than being Jewish or Gentile, your national identity, or being male or female. Other disciples are your people, your tribe. Disciples are representatives of the Messiah. When you see your fellow disciple, you should see Yeshua and feel starstruck.

Yeshua taught us that the commandment "Love your neighbor as yourself" applies to all human beings, but when it comes to disciples, that's not enough. Disciples must love one another more than our own lives:

> A new commandment I give to you, that you love one another: just as I have loved you, you also are to love one another. (John 13:34)

> By this we know love, that he laid down his life for us, and we ought to lay down our lives for our brothers. (1 John 3:16)

Make disciples of Yeshua your forever friends. These are your people. Be intentional about connecting with them and staying in touch.

SEPARATE

Connecting with other disciples is not enough. We also need boundaries. You will have secular friends, and you should. You must always be kind and loving to others, no matter who they are. Greet everyone with a smile. But when push comes to shove, there is a difference between you and them because you are a child of light.

You will become like the people around you. This is a simple fact of human psychology. Don't kid yourself into thinking that you're immune to this. If you spend most of your social life with secular people, you will begin to think like them. You will act like them. They will shape your sense of what is normal.

This means that there is a level of intimacy that we cannot cross with secular friends. Carrying out your mission in this world requires healthy boundaries. Have secular friends, but keep them at a safe distance, and carefully ration the time you spend with them. The people you pour your life into should be fellow disciples—and not disciples in name only. Find friends who will challenge you to increase in holiness.

DISTINCT

Now that you're drawing close to other disciples and creating a healthy distance from secular people, you have another task as a child of light: living a life of holiness. To learn what this means, let's look at Ephesians 5.

"Therefore be imitators of God, as beloved children." In other words, if we are God's children, we should copy what he does. "Walk in love, as Christ loved us and gave himself up for us, a fragrant offering and sacrifice to God." As I explained, our love for fellow disciples must be even greater than the level of "love your neighbor as yourself." Disciples give their lives for one another.

"But sexual immorality and all impurity or covetousness must not even be named among you, as is proper among saints. Let there be no filthiness nor foolish talk nor crude joking, which are out of place, but instead let there be thanksgiving." Everything Paul lists for disciples to avoid describes the secular world in a nutshell. It is the same today as it was 2,000 years ago. The secular world has no concept of sexual morality or boundaries. Even though this causes incredible harm to people personally, and difficulties for society, they have no concept of how to fix it. The Bible clearly states that for disciples, sexual contact of any kind must happen only between a husband and wife.

"Impurity" represents the lack of boundaries. In the Torah, impurity comes from contact with death. As children of light, we are always careful about what we come in contact with, knowing that everything that touches us affects us. "Covetousness," wanting what other people have, is rampant in the secular world. These are all things we must guard against as children of light.

"For you may be sure of this, that everyone who is sexually immoral or impure, or who is covetous (that is, an idolater), has no inheritance in the kingdom of Christ and God." Our goal is to receive the inheritance of the kingdom. Do not throw this inheritance away due to influences from society.

"Let no one deceive you with empty words, for because of these things the wrath of God comes upon the sons of disobedience." In other words, secular culture will try to convince you that none of these things are that big of a deal, even while it is collapsing under their weight.

"Therefore do not associate with them; for at one time you were darkness, but now you are light in the Lord. Walk as children of light (for the fruit of light is found in all that is good and right and true), and try to discern what is pleasing to the Lord."

YOUR STRATEGY

How is it possible to maintain the light in a society full of darkness? We learn from the example of the Israelites and the Passover lamb that we have to do three things. First, make lifetime connections with other disciples of Yeshua. Learn from them, study with them, and teach them. Second, stay separate from the rest of society, not becoming partners with them, and not letting them define our concept of normal because we are from a different world. And third, remain distinct in holiness, imitating God and staying pure.

This doesn't mean you become a hermit, never coming out of your house or never befriending other people. Build a healthy social circle with other disciples; this will equip you to be more effective in reaching out. You will be protected, and you will be able to shine your light.

Put effort into building lifetime bonds with other disciples. If you don't have a *chavruta*—a study partner—find one. Find someone you will continue to study with regularly. You can have more than one *chavruta*; even a long-distance *chavruta* can work well. Take advantage of the miracles of our high-tech era.

Once you've created those bonds, whether they are with a study partner or a friend, keep those people accountable. Check in with them and make sure you challenge each other to go further in godliness.

Make a list of the friends you hang out with. This is private, just for yourself. Categorize those people. Which ones are disciples? Which ones are secular? Which ones encourage you to grow in holiness, and which ones hold you back? Who are your mentors, your peers, and your students? Now that you've got this organized, strategically build the relationships that will help you most. Reinforce the boundaries in places where they are too relaxed.

When you are intentional with your relationships, you will become spiritually stronger, able to rescue others out of darkness and hold up the spiritually weak. If you just let the chips fall where they may, you will find yourself spiraling into the void of godlessness, sacrificing all the work you put into your connection with Yeshua.

By setting up boundaries in your relationships, you are no longer unprotected, like a burning log removed from a campfire. When you bind yourself to other disciples, you will become strong and bright like a lighthouse in a storm.

RELIGIOUS PRETENDER

But there is still a danger. Insulating yourself in a protected religious bubble doesn't make you a good person. In fact, you could wind up being a pretender. How do you keep that from happening? We'll talk about that in the next chapter.

CHAPTER 5

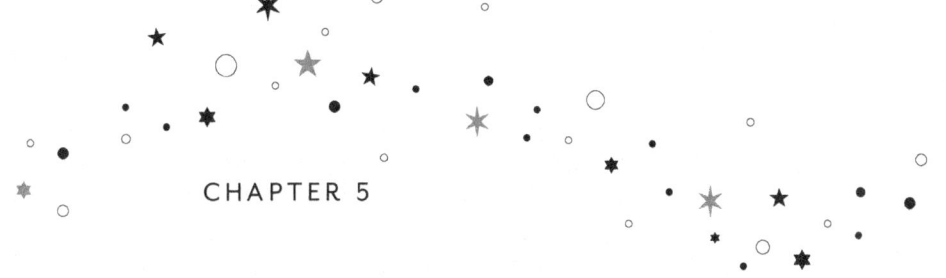

Perfect Light

Judaism teaches that everyone falls into three categories: the righteous, the wicked, and the in-between. I have two questions for you. First, in which of those groups are you? Second, how well are you doing in that category?

WHERE DO YOU STAND?

Chances are you consider yourself in the in-between crowd. You know you're not perfect, but you have good intentions, and in light of your personal struggles and challenges, you are doing okay.

If you answered that you are an in-between person who is doing pretty well considering the circumstances, I'm going to tell you that's the wrong way to see yourself. Let me explain what I mean.

Yeshua said, "You therefore must be perfect, as your heavenly Father is perfect" (Matthew 5:48). What is he talking about? How can a human be perfect like God is perfect? Once you make one mistake, you've failed, right? We need to clarify what our Master is expecting of us.

DIFFERENT

In the last chapter, we discussed the importance of separating ourselves from the darkness. As a child of light, being a disciple is the most important part of your identity. You need to forge deep bonds of friendship with other disciples. Find mentors to teach you, peers to challenge you, and students to raise up.

We have relationships with secular people, and we are commanded to love each person as ourselves, but we need to keep those secular relationships at arm's length. It is a fact of human psychology that you become like those with whom you spend time.

As children of light, it is our calling to conduct our lives in holiness. We stay away from any trace of sexual immorality. We need good boundaries to protect ourselves from negative influences. We guard our hearts against covetousness, wanting what other people have. We even guard our sense of humor because humor has the power to desensitize us to things that we usually recognize as wrong.

WAIT, WHY AM I DOING ALL THIS?

This is great! Now you are a spiritual person. You have surrounded yourself with other spiritual people who all do spiritual things together. You have separated yourself from negative influences and are no longer like the godless people in the secular world. You think you've reached your goal and are destined for the kingdom.

Well, think again. Your evil inclination has a new strategy. Being a religious person becomes like having a job. You get used to it, and you forget about the big picture—why this is your identity in the first place and what you are in this world to accomplish. It becomes a habit to be religious and to think that you're better than the outsiders.

You live a decent life, but are you perfect? No, you know very well that you'll never be perfect. That would be ridiculous. But how hard do you need to work to be considered "good"? You don't want to be bad, but subconsciously you might wonder, "What is the minimum I need to do to keep my status as a good person?"

There's an easy way to find out. You are surrounded by religious people. Their opinion of you seems like an obvious way to figure out how good you need to be and what you can get away with. If they see you as a good person, then you're doing fine. Why try harder than that?

Unfortunately—maybe conveniently for you—your fellow religious people can't see what is inside your heart. They have no idea what you do in private. The secret places in your mind and in your life can get yucky. But everyone else still admires you for being so righteous, which is nice. Congratulations, you have now become a pretender.

Maybe this dissonance bothers you. Or maybe it doesn't; maybe you prefer being able to get away with a lot of junk. You justify yourself because you are pretty sure everyone else is just as bad as you.

Maybe you get a lot of respect and validation from your peers. But if you think about it, is doing this religious stuff worth it? You're missing out on a lot just to maintain this image of being a religious person. When you look at the secular world, you feel deprived of the good things in life, and you're not sure you want to keep it up.

A spiritual community is supposed to encourage you to be authentic. But in this case, it's helping you maintain a charade. This is a problem. If you can't find authentic spirituality in the religious community, then where can you find it? How can you overcome the trap of "carnal spirituality"?

SOLD OUT

This is the real difference between a religious person and a child of light. Children of light are not looking to do the minimum to avoid getting into trouble. They are not just going through the motions; they know they are souls sent into this world on a mission to redeem it. Their identity revolves around godliness and the kingdom; every mitzvah, virtue, and spark of holiness in this world is precious to them.

The "pretender effect" is a temptation for everyone. But children of light conquer it by holding on to a kingdom perspective. They buy into the mission of bringing the kingdom, not just the job of being religious.

CHASSIDUT

One of Yeshua's sayings in the Sermon on the Mount is confusing for many Christian interpreters:

> Therefore whoever relaxes one of the least of these commandments and teaches others to do the same will be called least in the kingdom of heaven, but whoever does them and teaches them will be called great in the kingdom of heaven. For I tell you, unless your righteousness exceeds that of the scribes and Pharisees, you will never enter the kingdom of heaven. (Matthew 5:19-20)

Here's the problem: The scribes and Pharisees were strict Torah-keepers. Today people sometimes use Pharisee as an insult meaning "hypocrite." That's not what it means. When Yeshua says "Pharisee," he's talking about ordinary religious people; they were the kosher Orthodox Jews of his time.

Doesn't it seem unreasonable to tell us that we must be more righteous than the Pharisees to get into heaven? Also, someone might argue, we're not supposed to be able to earn our way to heaven by being righteous. That's being "saved by works." Some conclude, then, that the way to become more righteous than the Pharisees is not by doing good or keeping commandments. Instead, righteousness comes by becoming a Christian and receiving the righteousness of Jesus as a free gift. Our actions don't count at all.

The problem with this interpretation is that it misses Yeshua's point. He had just finished saying that we have to do and teach the commandments. Then he went on to explain specific ways in which the religious community was not keeping the commandments as well as they should. It makes no sense for him suddenly to say the commandments don't matter.

The passage makes more sense when we take it at face value. Yeshua really is telling us to be more righteous than the scribes and Pharisees—but not so we can go to heaven when we die. He's not talking about that; he's talking about entering the kingdom—bringing the Messianic Era. In other words, his point is that the standards of the religious community held at the time were not high enough to bring the redemption and the Messianic Age.

But we still have this question: How can we be more righteous than people who were extremely scrupulous in their observance? Yeshua's teaching aims to give us the tools to bring the Messianic Era. One of the main things he teaches is a concept called *chassidut*. Let's see how this will help us understand what he wants from us.

You may have heard the term *chassidut*, or *Chassidus*, in reference to a specific Jewish sect, the folks with long *peyot* (sidelocks) and black hats. But the word *chassidut* already meant something before they came along. *Chassidut* is a character trait. *Chassidut* is a passion for what you do that makes you strive for the highest level. When you behave with *chassidut*, you don't cut corners. You are not satisfied with attaining a minimum standard because you believe what you do is important.

When people are dedicated and passionate like this, others might think of them as exceptional heroes. But Yeshua teaches that this dedication, *chassidut*, isn't only for exceptional heroes. He teaches that the way to bring the kingdom is for this passion to be normal.

THE TORAH'S TWO JOBS

What confuses people about keeping the Torah is that the Torah is trying to accomplish two things at once. On the one hand, the Torah is a legal framework for society. It provides the structure (for the Jewish people especially) to build a civilization, live together, and work out interpersonal conflicts. It sets up a system of courts of law and enforcement and legislation, and it entrusts us to govern one another. It tells us what to do with people who break laws.

The second thing that the Torah does is reveal the will and wisdom of God. It is the light of the world. It shows each person who God is and how to seek him. The Torah is guidance not just for society at large but for each person on how to judge their own hearts.

For example, the Torah tells us not to murder. If someone does murder another person, and there are witnesses who saw it happen, then those witnesses must testify before a court of law. If their testimony holds up, then the murderer is executed.

This shows society what to do about a murderer. This is the legal part of the Torah. But on a deeper level, the Torah teaches us to value one another's life. It tells us not to harbor grudges. It instructs us to love one another as ourselves. This is God's will and wisdom. This is the light of the world.

You can't call the police or go to court and complain, "My neighbor does not love me as himself." According to Torah, you might be 100 percent right, and your neighbor is a lawbreaker. But there is no way to enforce that on a legal level. This is something between them and God. We each must judge and enforce Torah on that level for ourselves.

Look at what Moses taught:

> Now, Israel, what does the LORD your God require of you, but to fear the LORD your God, to walk in all his

ways, to love him, to serve the LORD your God with all your heart and with all your soul, and to keep the commandments and statutes of the LORD, which I am commanding you today for your good? (Deuteronomy 10:12-13)

Moses explained that serving God requires five things:

1. Fear of God
2. Walking in his ways
3. Loving God
4. Perfecting your heart
5. Keeping the commandments

Fear of God is the awareness of God and the understanding that you will be punished and rewarded for your deeds. Walking in his ways means imitating him, which includes character traits such as being merciful and generous to others. Loving God means a stirring in your heart that you want God to be happy; you want to serve him just so that he is pleased. Perfecting your heart means your service is for pure and right reasons, not out of habit, but out of devotion. And finally, keeping the commandments is just what it sounds like: keeping the external rules laid out in the Torah.

Being Torah observant requires five things, and four of them are internal. Only the last one, keeping the commandments, is external. The Torah is 20 percent external and 80 percent internal.

The Torah has two purposes: the external purpose, which tells us how to operate as a society, and the internal purpose, which shows us how to devote ourselves to the love and service of God.

The problem is that a person can be good enough externally that no one can take them to court or convict them of a crime, and they might think this means they are a good person. But it does not. If you ace the 20 percent that's on the outside but fail on the

80 percent that's on the inside, you are, as the medieval sage Nachmanides wrote, "corrupt with the permission of Torah."

PRETENDING

Yeshua focuses on this teaching: that the Torah has an external component that others can see and judge but also has an internal component that only we can judge for ourselves until it's time for God to judge us. No one else can see our inner observance of Torah, so other people might think we're righteous even if we neglect the 80 percent that's inside. Other people's approval fools us into thinking that the internal Torah is less important or only for exceptionally righteous people. But Yeshua teaches not only that it's just as important but also that we won't see the kingdom without it.

This was Yeshua's primary message to the religious community because it was their most prominent area of failure. He words it harshly in Matthew 23.

In this scathing rebuke, he calls the religious leaders of his day "hypocrites." This word comes up a lot in the Gospels, but it's not quite correct translation of what Yeshua said. A hypocrite is someone who tells others to do something but doesn't do it themselves. For example, if I tell you to share with others, but I don't want to share with anyone, I'm a hypocrite. That's bad, but it's not the problem Yeshua was addressing.

The word translated as "hypocrites" should really be translated as "pretenders" or "performers" because it describes a person who acts spiritual only to impress others. Let's look at Yeshua's rebuke in Matthew 23:23, but we'll replace the word "hypocrites" with "pretenders":

> Woe to you, scribes and Pharisees, [pretenders]! For you tithe mint and dill and cumin, and have neglected

the weightier matters of the law: justice and mercy and faithfulness. These you ought to have done, without neglecting the others.

Here we see that the observant Jews of his time were strict about tithing. Tithing in the Torah is different from what many churches teach about tithing today. When food is grown in the land of Israel, it has special holiness. The Torah requires Jews to take a part of that food and give it to the priests—the *kohanim*. Until you take out that part and tithe it, none of it is kosher. If you buy food at the store, and it was grown in Israel, you might not know if it's been tithed yet. So the Pharisees were scrupulous about tithing everything they bought just in case it hadn't been tithed yet. They were careful even with things like spices that the Torah doesn't say you have to tithe.

Yeshua said to them, "It's great that you do that; there's nothing wrong with being careful about tithing. But you are missing the point of the Torah; you're not seeing the light of the world contained within the Torah. The Torah guides us to be just and merciful and faithful. Those are internal things others might not see or give you credit for." Look at what he said next:

> You blind guides, straining out a gnat and swallowing a camel! (Matthew 23:24)

Here he's using a figure of speech. They find a tiny bug in their soup and take it out because it's not kosher. This is good, but then they swallow a camel. They are not literally eating camels, but they are doing things that are just as non-kosher. He goes on:

> Woe to you, scribes and Pharisees, [pretenders]! For you clean the outside of the cup and the plate, but inside they are full of greed and self-indulgence. You blind Pharisee! First clean the inside of the cup and the plate, that the outside also may be clean. (Matthew 23:25-26)

Yeshua is talking about dunking dishes in a mikvah, a ritual pool, to purify them. The rule is that the water must touch the entire surface of the dish. If you wash a cup and put it in the water with the open side down, when you pull it back out again, the inside won't be wet because of the trapped air inside. It looks like it was dunked on the outside, but the water never touched the inside, so the dish is not actually pure. Yeshua is making the same point again. He's telling them that if you keep the external Torah but ignore the internal Torah, you are not Torah observant. You are pretending. You're like a cup dunked upside down:

> Woe to you, scribes and Pharisees, [pretenders]! For you are like whitewashed tombs, which outwardly appear beautiful, but within are full of dead people's bones and all uncleanness. So you also outwardly appear righteous to others, but within you are full of [pretense] and lawlessness. (Matthew 23:27–28)

We see how important it is to Yeshua to keep Torah on the inside and not just on the outside. But the external Torah is so much easier. It gives you immediate rewards because other people can see it. And it is easy to measure and know if you are up to snuff. The internal Torah is harder.

SELF-IMPROVEMENT

To learn the external Torah, you can study halachah. Halachah is the rules and technicalities about how to keep the commandments. By studying halachah, you can learn the dos and don'ts of Shabbat. You can learn how to make kosher food. Halachah is an integral part of the Torah. It tells us what someone can and can't do. But it doesn't say much about what someone should do. If you've learned halachah, you have only learned one-fifth of the Torah. The outside fifth.

How do you learn the four-fifths on the inside? What is the process for becoming a keeper of the internal Torah? The best way to do this is through a kind of Jewish study known as musar. Musar literally means "discipline." It is often used to refer to the study of ethics and self-improvement in Judaism.

Most books about musar are based on lists of character traits. The Hebrew word for character traits is *middot*. Some examples of good *middot* are honesty, patience, and gratitude.

Often, these *middot* follow a natural progression. For example, one of the sages in the Talmud explained:

> Rabbi Pinchas ben Ya'ir would say: Torah study leads to carefulness in the performance of mitzvot. Carefulness in the performance of mitzvot leads to diligence in their observance. Diligence leads to cleanliness of the soul. Cleanliness leads to separating from bad influences. Separation leads to purity. Purity leads to dedication. Dedication leads to humility. Humility leads to fear of sin. Fear of sin leads to holiness. Holiness leads to the Holy Spirit. The Holy Spirit leads to the resurrection of the dead. (b.*Avodah Zarah* 20b)

This list follows a logical path. One of the most famous musar books, *Mesillat Yesharim*, "*The Path of the Just*," uses this list as an outline and goes into detail about what each trait is, why it is important, and how to cultivate it in your life. I highly recommend reading this book or any book on musar. Our own apostles gave us musar. If you look closely, you'll see that most of the books in the New Testament contain musar lessons. The trick is to recognize them and apply them to your life.

For example, the letter of 2 Peter supplies us with a list of important *middot*:

> For this very reason, make every effort to supplement your faith with virtue, and virtue with knowledge, and knowledge with self-control, and self-control with steadfastness, and steadfastness with godliness, and godliness with brotherly affection, and brotherly affection with love. For if these qualities are yours and are increasing, they keep you from being ineffective or unfruitful in the knowledge of our [Master Yeshua the Messiah]. (2 Peter 1:5-8)

Study each of these *middot*, learn what it is, and make sure that it characterizes your life.

THE KINGDOM PERSPECTIVE

As a child of light, your primary interest in life is to gain the hidden light. This world and all its rewards are nothing in comparison, including praise from your peers for acting religious. Our eyes are set on the World to Come. That means we need to keep 100 percent of the Torah that applies to us, not just the 20 percent that other people can see.

The entire reason God gives us a few decades here on earth with our souls trapped in meat robots is to go through the process of self-improvement. This is our opportunity to grow and become perfect. Being perfect doesn't mean we never make mistakes. It means becoming the person God made you to be. Step by step, day by day, we are supposed to improve. This is what Yeshua meant when he said, "You therefore must be perfect, as your heavenly Father is perfect" (Matthew 5:48).

At the beginning of the chapter, I said that people fall into three categories: the righteous, the wicked, and the in-between. Maybe you thought of yourself as an in-between person who is doing pretty well under the circumstances. But I told you that's not the right way to see yourself.

When you pray, when you give, when you love, when you serve others, when you have faith, when you show self-control, what kind of expectations do you place upon yourself? Do you hold yourself up to the standard of a pretty good in-between person?

God did not put you on earth to be in-between. That is not your mission in life. You are a tzaddik, a righteous person. That is your identity and your job description. With every task and decision in life, you should ask, what would a tzaddik—an extremely righteous person, inside and out—do in this situation?

Once you understand that this is what you are called to, you can't see yourself as an in-between person doing reasonably well. Instead, if you're like me, you will realize that you are a righteous person who is doing poorly. The point isn't to feel guilty but to see what you should aspire to and not let yourself think you've arrived.

STOP PRETENDING

As children of light, we refuse to be pretenders. But the evil inclination likes to make us focus more on the outside than on the inside. It makes us think that as long as our religious friends think we're righteous, we don't need to worry about improving ourselves. We have to fix this.

Step one is to have a kingdom perspective. We've talked about how this life is just the admission line. Our real reward is waiting for us in the next world.

The second step is to buy into the mission and not just the job. Being a godly person is not like working at Wal-Mart, wearing a uniform, clocking in and clocking out, or getting through the to-do list. We are doing this because of our love and fear of God and hope for the future. We believe it is the right thing to do, so we put everything into it.

The third step is to improve ourselves, to live out the 80 percent of the Torah that is unseen. Perfection doesn't mean you're never allowed to fail; it means you never stop working to improve. If we do these things, we will not fall into the trap of becoming pretenders.

Identify one character trait you can improve today that no one else will know about. You might be able to think of a few, but I want you to focus on one for now. Research what this character trait means, why it's important, and how to live it out.

For pretenders, religious life is a chore they will put up with only as long as there are people around to impress. When those kudos go away, they lose interest and sink back into worldliness.

But that's not you. You are pursuing the perfection of your soul and the kingdom of heaven. If you break free of being a pretender, you will become a true child of light, headed for the kingdom and its rewards—the revelation of God.

CHAPTER 6

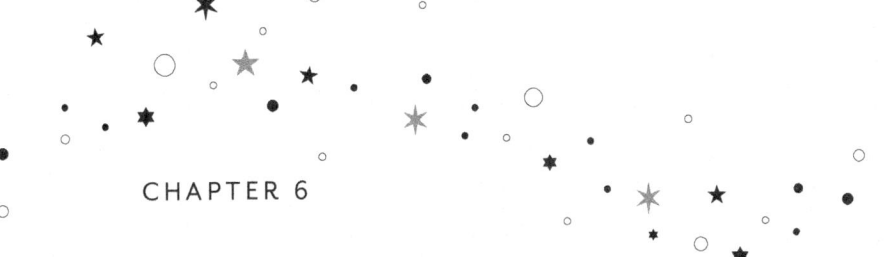

Basking in the Light

God created the world, the universe, vast beyond comprehension, full of galaxies and stars, all for us. He infused this world with light—not just physical light, but the light of revelation: the why and how of everything. He made this light for us. But he wanted to preserve our free will, our power to choose, so he had to hide that light and save it for us in the future.

CHANNELING THE LIGHT

In the meantime, it's our job to seek him, following the rays that beam into our universe: the Torah, the Temple, Shabbat, and the Messiah. We cling to Yeshua because he guides the way to our inheritance: the hidden light.

As children of light, we are supposed to be a channel of light for the rest of the world. To do this without distorting this pure light, we must become nothing, transparent. We need to nullify ourselves and behave with humility.

We face many dangers along the way. The world is dark, and it draws us into that darkness. So we band together as disciples, supporting one another, learning from one another, and encouraging one another. We try to bring light into the dark world, but we need to keep the world at a safe distance.

Even in the safe space we create, there is another danger. It's easy for complacency to set in, threatening to reduce our spirituality to mere habits. We're tempted to do just enough to get approval from our peers even as we let our inner self rot and decay. To keep that from happening, we embark on self-improvement, focusing our eyes on the kingdom and seeking perfection.

FALLING SHORT

Now here you are; you want to succeed in your mission to experience and reveal God's light in the world. You have broken free from religious pretending, and your eyes are focused on the kingdom. You want nothing more.

But it's not so easy. You find that the things you thought you had conquered haven't gone away. Not only that, but it also feels as if life is stacked against you: your physical, finite lizard brain; the natural universe; your own animalistic tendencies; the godless surrounding culture; and your hypocritical ego. It turns out that you haven't conquered any of these enemies. They won't stop attacking, and you constantly fall short.

You don't see concrete evidence of God. Even if you did, would your brain even comprehend it? Your faith falters. You don't have the self-discipline or time to memorize whole chapters of the Bible like the Sermon on the Mount, the core teaching of the Messiah you claim to follow.

No matter how hard you try, you can't stop being human; you sometimes give in to your impulses and do what feels good, even when you know it's wrong. The culture still rubs off on you, desensitizing you to immorality.

Even though you know in your mind that it's all about the kingdom, sometimes you know you're putting on a religious persona to hide the darkness inside you. You are supposed to be perfect? A tzaddik? That's expecting the impossible.

Maybe you feel like a failure. You feel angry at yourself for not living up to your own expectations and angry at God for not revealing himself more or making it easier for you. Why would God create faulty humans and then ask them to do something they are incapable of doing? It's not fair for him to judge you for failing to do something impossible.

Every one of us feels this inadequacy because we all continually fall short of God's demands on our lives. But there is a way for you to overcome the enormity of the task God gave you.

This is the most critical part of this book. If you only take one idea away, I want it to be the message I have for you in this chapter.

GOD NEEDS YOU

Human beings are not like other creatures on this planet. We are the only creatures that can contemplate our own existence. We are not in creation; we are creation. And we are the only way for creation to know its creator.

This is because God made us in his image. It was an act of love for him to make us in his image, and it was an act of love for him to reveal it to us. He didn't have to.

Our faith teaches that humans are not an accident. You are a soul, a spark of godliness, God's own precious treasure that originated in heaven. You were sent to earth on a dangerous mission. It was not a mere chance that you were born the person you are. As the Ba'al Shem Tov once said, the day you were born was the day God decided the world could not exist without you. HaShem loves you. He didn't put you in this universe to fail, but instead to accomplish your purpose.

HaShem doesn't just love you; he needs you. You might think that you need HaShem, but that's not true. You don't need anything; you don't even need to exist. You didn't decide to exist. HaShem wanted and needed you so much that he decided to put you in this world and give you everything. The simple fact that you were created is proof that God loves you.

You might think that you are no good, that you've already failed, that God has already given up on you. This is entirely false. You have a mission and purpose in life for as long as you are alive. When God decides you are no longer capable or needed in this world, you will stop breathing. If you are breathing right now, that means you can accomplish his purpose for you. HaShem loves you and wants you to succeed.

WHAT IS LOVE?

In its purest form, love is the expression of who God is. The essence of love is selfless giving. The universe continues to exist only because of God's constant act of selfless giving.

In humans, love comes from our sense of self and our own desire to exist. When you give something to someone else, whether you give something physical, your time, or your emotional energy, the other person now has a part of you. You have invested in them, and because you care about yourself, and they now have a little bit of you, you care about them. That's how love works.

Have you ever given someone a gift and wanted so badly to see them enjoy it? Have you ever prayed for someone? The more you do that, especially if you make it a regular habit, the more you begin to care about how they are doing. This also happens with animals. The more you take care of a pet, the more you will love it, and the sadder you will be when it dies. This is even true with plants or projects. You don't give to someone because you love them. You love them because you give. You love yourself, and when you give, you love the "you" that is now invested in the other person.

That is why the Torah commands us, "Love your neighbor as yourself." Loving yourself is automatic. When you see your neighbor as a part of you, you will love them, too.

God built this principle into the universe. Now think about this: Before the universe existed, there was only God. God created the universe because he wanted to love. For God to love something, something other than him needs to exist. So he made a universe with humans in it. Humans are in his image because that is the optimal way for us to receive his love. He gave us everything that exists. If you love your plant because you water it every day, think about how much God loves you. He invented the laws of physics and brought galaxies into existence just so you would exist and live right now. Love is a pure expression of God because love is giving, and giving is what God does to his world.

As children of light, we are children of God. We imitate God. Love is in our nature:

> Beloved, let us love one another, for love is from God, and whoever loves has been born of God and knows God. Anyone who does not love does not know God, because God is love. (1 John 4:7-8)

Not only has God loved us by giving us life, but he is also eager to give us the greatest gift of all: the hidden light. That is why he has sent us glimmers of that light in the meantime: the Torah, the Temple, Shabbat, and Yeshua the Messiah:

> In this the love of God was made manifest among us, that God sent his only Son into the world, so that we might live through him. In this is love, not that we have loved God but that he loved us and sent his Son to be the propitiation for our sins. Beloved, if God so loved us, we also ought to love one another. No one has ever seen God; if we love one another, God abides in us and his love is perfected in us. (1 John 4:9-12)

God proved his love for you when he sent Yeshua into this world to guide you to the hidden light. He didn't send Yeshua because we are perfect enough to deserve him. He sent him because we make mistakes. This was his plan for turning those mistakes into redemptions.

HaShem is deeply invested in you. He has given you everything there is to give. He wants nothing more than for you to accomplish your purpose, overcome all your challenges, and gain the hidden light. HaShem loves you.

REACH OUT TO GOD

Maybe you are used to thinking of HaShem as a judge. As an authority figure who is critical of everything you do. Either as someone to be afraid of or as someone so busy ruling the world, he doesn't really pay attention to what you're doing.

HaShem is a king and a judge. We should fear him; we should honor him. We are his servants, and he is our master. We shouldn't forget that. Many people miss that and fail to treat HaShem with the respect and fear he deserves. But beyond all that, Yeshua taught us to relate to HaShem as our Abba, our Father who cares deeply about us.

We all go through difficult things in life. Some of us go through intensely painful things. That's because life is a test. Every moment of your life is a test. The difficult times are tests, and the easy times are also tests. The purpose of this world is to put your soul in various situations to test it and for your soul to overcome those tests.

Overcoming the tests doesn't mean solving the problems you face. It means making the right choice. Sometimes that choice is as simple as doing what you already know is right. Obey God's commands. Be a kind person. Resist the evil inclination and your animalistic urges.

But let's think about a different kind of choice. Life hands us messes. Sometimes we make those messes ourselves. In life, there is always something stressing you out. Whatever it is, tell your Abba in heaven about it and ask him for help.

Praying doesn't always have to be formal. Prayers from the Siddur—*Shacharit, Minchah, Ma'ariv*—are just one kind of prayer. They only scratch the surface of what prayer is. You have a relationship with God. You can just talk to him. You should talk to him.

When life presents challenges, our first instinct should be to cry out to God for help. We shouldn't think, *I got myself into this mess; I'll get myself out*. Nor should you assume that because God already knows what you need, it's pointless to call on him. Don't think, "I don't deserve to ask God for help now because I did not pray when things were going well." Your Abba in heaven is always eager to hear your prayers. Ask him for help. It's never the wrong time to talk to him.

Why is it important to ask God for help? Doesn't he already know we need help? Of course, but by asking him, we change ourselves. We admit that success and failure are not in our hands, nor are they a matter of random chance or fate. One of the greatest mistakes the Torah warns about is to think that the difficult things we are going through are random. When we think this way, we fail to recognize HaShem's control over everything in life.

It is critical to develop a reflex to rush to the Father in prayer any time we feel stress, whether our problems are personal or affecting our whole community.

Even Yeshua cried out to God for help when he felt stressed:

> In the days of his flesh, [Yeshua] offered up prayers and supplications, with loud cries and tears, to him who was able to save him from death, and he was heard because of his reverence. Although he was a son, he learned obedience through what he suffered. (Hebrews 5:7-8)

Sarah, Rebekah, Rachel, and Leah are the mothers of the Jewish people. Every one of them was unable to conceive a child without a miracle. Their destiny and greatest accomplishment—motherhood of the chosen nation—was something physically impossible for them to do.

This struggle was a significant source of stress in their lives. They cried. They lost sleep. They were mocked and made fun of for being childless. Why would God put them through this? The sages tell us it is because "HaShem longs for the prayers of the righteous." He wanted them to pray about it, which is what they did. They prayed intensely.

It is not that God enjoys our suffering, but when we choose to pray in times of difficulty, it transforms us and binds us to our Creator. When you pray year after year for a child, and then finally a miracle occurs, and the child is born, that child is the fruit of your struggle with God, and this experience changes the way you see that child.

Receiving a gift from God as an answer to fervent prayer is much more powerful than receiving a blessing out of nowhere.

PRAY ALWAYS

If you pray only when you are in trouble, it is infinitely better than not praying at all. But ideally, you should talk to him all the time about everything. God created you because he wanted someone to love. Your purpose in life is to engage in a relationship with God. That means that every moment you spend talking to him is a moment you fulfill your reason for existing. God is always there with you.

One of the most important verses of the Bible in Jewish thought is Psalm 16:8:

> I have set the LORD always before me; because he is at my right hand, I shall not be shaken.

How do you set God somewhere if he permeates the whole universe? You set him before you in your mind. Open your spiritual eyes to see that God is present in every single moment. This is how you avoid being shaken.

HaShem loves you. He created you to talk to him. So talk to him. It doesn't have to be fancy. You don't need to impress God with your vocabulary; the goal is open, simple communication with him. Think of yourself as a little child talking with your mom or dad. Just say what you're thinking.

If you don't have the words to pray, that's what you can pray about. Tell your heavenly Father that you can't think of what to say and why. If you feel inadequate or unworthy or overwhelmed, tell him that and ask him for help.

Thinking *I don't have time to pray* doesn't make sense. If you don't have time to stop what you are doing, that's okay. You don't have to bow your head, close your eyes, or fold your hands. Just talk, like you're talking with a friend.

THE HOLY SPIRIT

As disciples of Yeshua, we have access to another tool that will help us on our quest:

> I tell you, ask, and it will be given to you; seek, and you will find; knock, and it will be opened to you. For everyone who asks receives, and the one who seeks finds, and to the one who knocks it will be opened. What father among you, if his son asks for a fish, will instead of a fish give him a serpent; or if he asks for an egg, will give him a scorpion? If you then, who are evil, know how to give good gifts to your children, how much more will the heavenly Father give the Holy Spirit to those who ask him! (Luke 11:9–13)

Have you ever tried to accomplish a task without the right tool? Say you need to turn a screw, but when you look around for a screwdriver, all you can find is a pen, so you stick the pen in there to try to catch the screwhead. Not only is it completely ineffective, but you're likely to break the pen and spill ink everywhere.

HaShem has a job for you: to prepare yourself and this world for his kingdom. We humans are fragile, fallible, easily fooled, and subject to animalistic impulses and instincts. It's a big job, but we don't have to do it without the proper tools. Yeshua tells us that if we ask, we can receive an important tool: the Holy Spirit. The Holy Spirit is the presence of God that inhabits our lives like the glory of God inhabited the Tabernacle. The Holy Spirit gives us a level of spiritual insight and supernatural strength.

HaShem wants you to have this tool. But Yeshua teaches that it doesn't come automatically. To receive the Holy Spirit, you must ask, seek, and knock. You must beat down HaShem's door and keep on asking. HaShem will answer, "No, the Holy Spirit is not for this age; it is reserved for the Messianic Era." But Yeshua teaches us not to accept that answer. We are supposed to argue back to HaShem that we need it now. Tell him, "I am a child of the Messianic Era. The Messiah is with me now. I can't afford to wait until the redemption!" Yeshua urges us to keep asking until we receive it.

Why do we have to ask so fervently and keep on persisting? If we need the Holy Spirit, why doesn't he just give it to us? It's the same reason Sarah, Rebekah, Rachel, and Leah were unable to have children. Wrestling with God is an essential part of our mission. Receiving the Holy Spirit must be the culmination of yearning, asking, reaching out, communicating, longing, believing, trusting, and clinging. You can't give up after five minutes or hours or days or years and say, "I've already asked and didn't get an answer."

YOUR PURPOSE

I'm going to say it again: HaShem loves you. You are not accidentally here. HaShem created you because you have a purpose in this world. He is rooting for you and wants you to achieve that purpose. Love is the act of selfless giving. That is what HaShem did in creating the universe, in creating you. His essence is entirely love.

You were created to experience a relationship with HaShem. He is your father, and you are his child. Every moment of this life is a test, including this moment you are experiencing now. Your purpose is to overcome each test you face. The most important test you face is the choice you make every moment of the day to seek HaShem. Reach out to him. Cry out to him. Know he's there. Ask him for help. Tell him what's on your mind. Let him know what you're thankful for.

Often, HaShem puts us through difficulties specifically so we keep reaching out to him. The result we get from crying out to him is better than it would be if he had simply given it to us. Even Yeshua had to endure this kind of suffering and pleading with God.

Yeshua teaches us that we should especially ask him for the Holy Spirit. The Holy Spirit is essential for us in our mission to bring the kingdom of heaven.

Don't worry if you haven't reached out to him before, and don't think you are unworthy of his love. His love is not based on our worthiness. He created you to be loved by him.

Spend some time today being very blunt with God. Tell him what you're frustrated about or even angry at him about. Tell him what you hope for your life and be honest with him about how you have failed to meet your own expectations of yourself. Ask him for help.

If you can't bring yourself to do that, or if you are not even sure God is listening, just say this: "Abba, help me. Abba, show yourself to me." Say it and mean it and watch for an answer.

If you don't turn to God for help and make this relationship your primary goal, you will find it impossible to maintain the façade of a spiritual life. You will be a body without a soul.

You don't have to keep struggling to keep your head above water, unable to stay true to a life of faith. Starting now, you are in constant conversation with God, and your struggles and difficulties are simply another reason for you to cry out to him.

You will achieve your true purpose: a relationship with God. When you cry out to God, he will help you. It is not through your own efforts but with his help. It will take your lifetime to accomplish it, but that makes sense because forging this relationship is your life's purpose.

CONCLUSION

This book explored some mind-blowing, mystical ideas and practical advice for daily living. I've taken you on a journey from creation itself to your personal circumstances and choices today. But finishing this book is not the end of the journey; it's just the beginning.

We learned that you are a child of light, and your inheritance is the light of creation. Your soul must go through the experiences of life to become the person God made you to be, but this presents an enormous challenge. You are limited and distracted by your own physical needs and desires, and the darkness around you is trying to overcome you. You must tap into the lights that break into this world. The greatest of these lights is the Messiah. Being his disciple means taking on his identity and making his mission into your mission. To be authentic, you need to get your personal agenda and need for recognition out of the way. Become transparent so others can see the light of Messiah shining through you.

To prevent the world from eroding your identity, you must connect with other disciples and keep worldly influences at a distance. But there is still the danger of becoming a pretender, of doing just enough to get by in your religious, social bubble. To fight this, you must be sold out for the mission. Instead of merely doing what others will see, let the Torah transform your inner self. This is hard work, and to succeed, you must stay in constant conversation with God, asking for his help every step of the way.

It's easy to lose sight of our identity and mission. If you are on a long and challenging journey, you must look at a roadmap and ensure you haven't taken a wrong turn. If you have, you must figure out how to get going back in the right direction. It's the same with our spiritual quest through life. We need to revisit these ideas regularly by reading the Bible, learning musar, and plugging into sources of inspiration and instruction that keep our eyes on the destination. This book is one resource you can re-read to remind yourself why God put you on this planet. As I spent time focusing on and articulating these ideas, it was a transformative experience for me. It reignited my own fervor for living as a child of light.

Whatever your life has been like until now, today is a fresh chance to embrace your identity as a child of light. This is your story, and you start writing it now. Today you can take a step toward your inheritance, the hidden light. I hope you are inspired and challenged to keep your eyes on a prize greater than anything the world can offer. I want to bless you and myself that God would give us strength and that we would not look for the fleeting pleasures of this world. With God's help, we will be able to say, "I have fought the good fight, I have finished the race, I have kept the faith" (2 Timothy 4:7).